The Secret Power Of Being You

A Guided Kids Journal For Understanding Your Feelings
& Becoming Your Best Self

Mimi Novic

Aspiring Hope
Publishing

Copyright © Mimi Novic 2025

All Rights Reserved. No part of this publication may be reproduced, stored in a retrieval system, or transmitted in any form or by any means, electronic, mechanical, photocopy, recording, or otherwise, without prior written permission from the copyright owner. Nor can it be circulated in any form of binding or cover other than that in which it is published, and without similar conditions, including this condition being imposed on a subsequent purchaser.
British Library Cataloguing Publication Data.
A catalogue record for this book is available from the British Library.
ISBN 9781068684883 Published by Aspiring Hope Publishing.

Disclaimer
The information and guidance provided in this book are intended to support children, parents, and caregivers in understanding and navigating emotions. While this book offers helpful insights and practical tips, it is not a substitute for professional medical or psychological advice.

If you or your child are experiencing significant emotional distress or mental health issues, we encourage you to seek the assistance of a qualified mental health professional. Every individual's emotional journey is unique, and professional guidance may be necessary for addressing specific concerns.

The authors and publishers of this book are not liable for any adverse effects or consequences resulting from the use or application of the information contained herein. This book is meant to serve as a resource for fostering emotional awareness and strength, but it is important to approach emotional well-being with care and professional support when needed.

About The Author

Mimi Novic is one of today's bestselling inspirational authors and is ranked amongst the top names in inspirational, motivational and spiritual books in the world. Her writings and quotes are considered some of the most popular in modern times and are used by some of today's most well known and influential figures.

She is internationally known as one of the most respected and highly regarded motivational and self awareness teachers in the fields of self-development. Her expertise has made her amongst the most popular and highly demanded well being experts of today. Working as a complementary medical practitioner, psychotherapist, self development teacher, voiceover artist and author, her collaborations with renowned experts across various disciplines underscore her commitment to delivering unparalleled experiences in personal growth. Mimi has collaborated with the most esteemed therapists, Grammy nominated composers, musicians, professors, healers and professionals in their field while bringing together powerful teams that work in synchronicity to bring the best possible life enhancing experiences for her patients and clients.

She is known for her work with high profile personalities and her engagements with notable and influential figures further attest to her ability to navigate the intersections of success and wellness. She teaches and runs workshops and seminars in a wide array of therapies, complementary medicine and self-awareness, working around the world in clinics, retreats and on a one to one basis.

For more information about Mimi Novic's inspirational work visit www.miminovic.co.uk

This Book Raises Funds For:

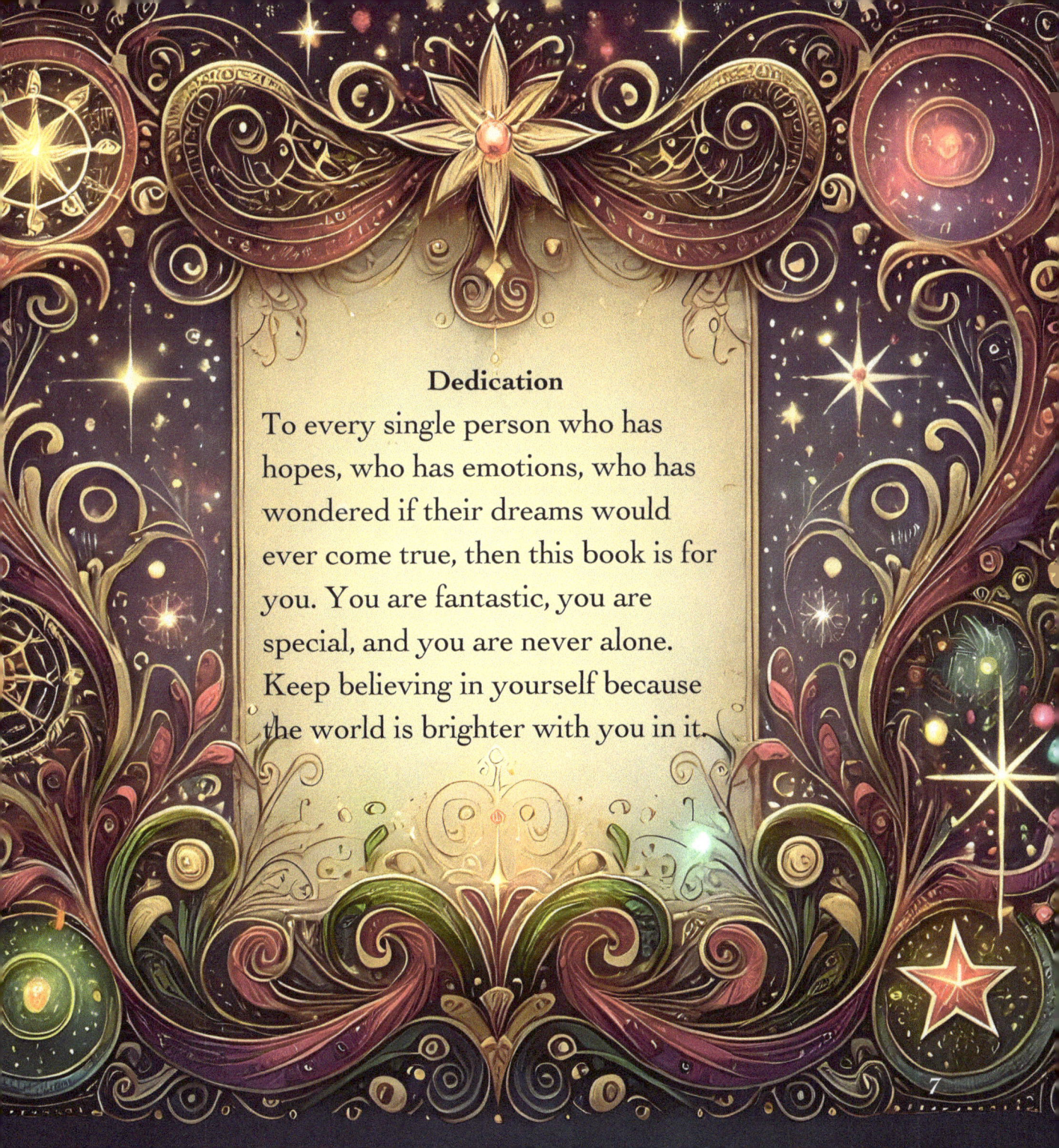

Dedication

To every single person who has hopes, who has emotions, who has wondered if their dreams would ever come true, then this book is for you. You are fantastic, you are special, and you are never alone. Keep believing in yourself because the world is brighter with you in it.

INDEX

Chapter 1: Finding Light On A Cloudy Day   15
  (For When You are Feeling Sad)

Chapter 2: Calm In The Storm   41
  (For When You Are Feeling Worried Or Anxious)

Chapter 3: Brave & Strong   67
  (For When You Are Feeling Scared)

Chapter 4: You Are Enough   93
  (For When You Are Feeling Insecure Or Not Good Enough)

Chapter 5: Finding Peace When You Are Upset   119
  (For When You Are Feeling Angry Or Overwhelmed)

Chapter 6: A Heart Full Of Gratitude   145
  (For When You Need To Focus On The Good)

INDEX

Chapter 7: Confidence Begins Within   171
  (For When You Are Feeling Unsure Of Yourself)

Chapter 8: Bouncing Back   197
  (For When You Are Dealing With Mistakes Or Disappointment)

Chapter 9: You Are Loved, Just As You Are   223
  (For When You Are Feeling Lonely Or Left Out)

Chapter 10: Dream Big, Shine Bright   249
  (For When You Need Motivation & Inspiration)

Chapter 11: Mindfulness, Relaxation & Meditation   275
  (For When You Need To Calm Down)

Wellbeing Tips   301

Introduction

Welcome, Amazing You!
Have you ever had a day where your feelings felt too big? Maybe you woke up feeling sad for no clear reason, or a small worry kept growing bigger in your mind. Perhaps you felt left out, upset, or like you just weren't good enough.

Guess what? You Are Not Alone
Every single person, kids, grown-ups, even the most confident and successful people, experiences moments like this. Everyone has days when they feel uncertain, anxious, or overwhelmed. But here's something important to remember: your feelings don't define you, and they don't last forever.

That's why this book exists. It's here to remind you that no matter what you are going through, you are strong, capable, and worthy of love and happiness. The emotions you feel right now are just a small part of your journey. They don't control you, and they don't decide your future.

But this isn't just any book; it's a toolbox for your emotions. Inside, you will find encouragement, wisdom, and simple, practical strategies to help you understand and manage your feelings. Each chapter is designed to match a specific emotion, so whenever you're feeling anxious, sad, or overwhelmed, you can turn to the section that speaks to you, take a deep breath, and let the words support you.

Because here's the truth: your emotions are not problems to fix; they are messages to understand. They tell you what matters to you. They remind you of your strengths and your needs. And the more you learn to listen to them, the better you'll understand yourself.

Introducing The Emotion Wheel

Before we begin this new adventure of discovering the real you, let us talk about a powerful tool you can use every day: the Emotion Wheel.
Imagine a colourful circle divided into different sections, each representing a different feeling: happiness, sadness, worry, excitement, loneliness, peace; it's all there.

The Emotion Wheel helps you recognise and name your feelings instead of letting them overwhelm you. Whenever you check in with yourself, try looking at the section that matches your mood. This simple act of noticing your emotions can help you feel more in control.

And here's something really important to remember: all emotions are valid. There are no wrong emotions. Feeling sad doesn't mean something is wrong with you. Feeling worried doesn't mean you're weak. Every feeling has a purpose. And when you acknowledge them, you give yourself the power to move forward with understanding and self-compassion.

What You Will Find Inside

This book is filled with ideas to help you through difficult moments. Inside, you'll discover:
-Encouraging messages to help you understand and process your feelings.
- Powerful affirmations, short, positive statements that shift your thoughts in a healthier direction.
- Interactive reflections, including simple activities and journal prompts that encourage self-awareness and growth.

These aren't just words on a page. They are helpers that can help you feel better, stronger, and more in control of your emotions.

How Words Can Change The Way You Feel

You might be wondering: How can reading a book help me feel better?
Great question! The answer is simple: words are powerful.

The way you talk to yourself, inside your mind, shapes the way you see yourself and the world around you. If you tell yourself, "I can't do this," your brain will believe it. But if you say, "I am learning and growing," your brain will believe that, too.

That's why positive affirmations are such an important part of this book. The more you repeat kind, encouraging words to yourself, the stronger your confidence becomes. You train your mind to focus on possibilities instead of problems. You start to see setbacks as stepping stones instead of roadblocks. And little by little, those words become part of who you are.

This Book Is Your Friend

Think of this book as a friend you can turn to whenever you need support.
You don't have to read it from start to finish all at once. You don't have to remember everything in one go. Just open it when you need comfort, motivation, or a reminder of how incredible you are.

Some days, you might need a message of encouragement. Other days, you might want a simple breathing exercise to help you feel calmer. Whatever you need, this book is here for you.

Because the truth is, you are not your worries. You are so much more than you know. You are strong, brave, and growing every single day.
So, are you ready? Let's begin this journey together. Because no matter what, you've got this.

Opening Reflection

Sadness is a feeling we all experience, and it is okay to feel this way sometimes. Just like a cloudy day eventually clears, your emotions will shift, and brighter moments will come. Even in difficult times, small sparks of joy and hope are always around you. This chapter will help you find comfort, strength, and light when you need it most.

Emotion Wheel Activity

Now, take a moment to look at the section of the Emotion Wheel that represents how you feel right now. This can help you connect with your emotions and express them.

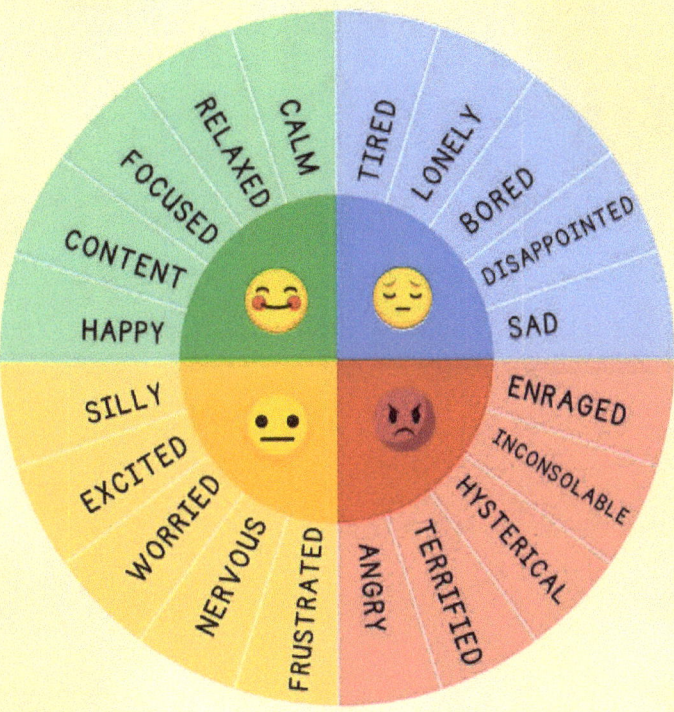

Positive Reminder:

Remember, sadness is just one part of your journey, and it is okay to feel this way. You have the strength to find light in even the cloudiest days.

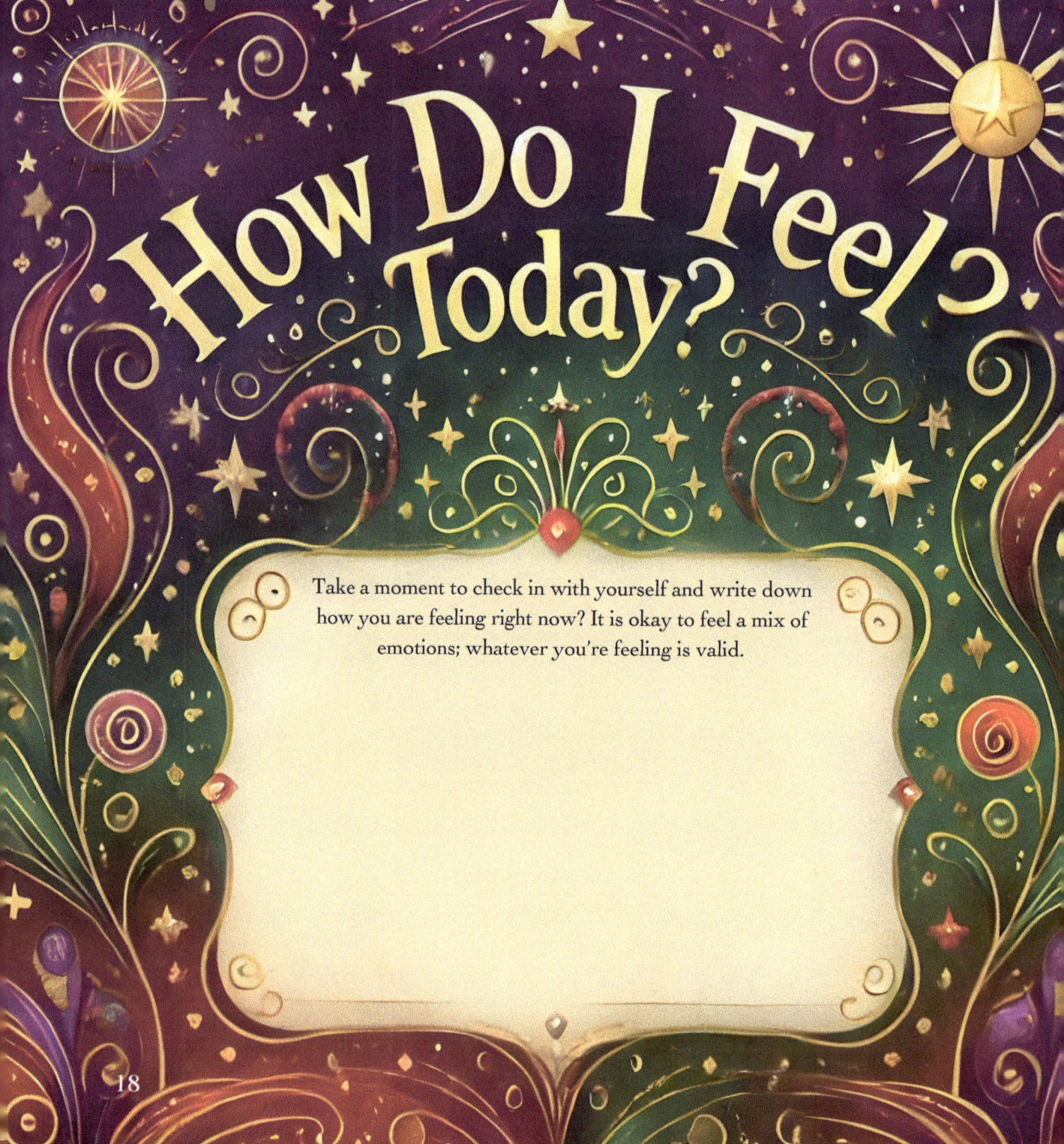

How Do I Feel Today?

Take a moment to check in with yourself and write down how you are feeling right now? It is okay to feel a mix of emotions; whatever you're feeling is valid.

POSITIVE THOUGHTS

Whenever you need a little encouragement, turn to these inspiring and powerful messages that will help you see the beauty in every moment. You'll learn how to turn challenges into stepping stones and discover the magic of believing in yourself.

Positive Thoughts

1. Emotions Are Like The Weather
Just as the sky changes from cloudy to sunny, feelings come and go. You may feel sad now, but this moment will pass. It is okay to sit with your feelings, knowing that happiness will return, just like the sun always does.

2. You Are Not Alone
Even when it feels like no one understands, there are people who care about you. Sometimes, sadness makes us want to be alone, but reaching out to someone you trust can make a world of difference.

3. Small Joys Can Bring Big Comfort
When sadness feels overwhelming, look for tiny moments of happiness, a warm hug, a favourite song, a kind word. These little things have the power to brighten your day, even just a little.

4. Tears Are Not Weakness
Crying is your body's way of letting go of heavy feelings. Just like the rain nourishes the earth, tears can help you feel lighter and ready for new beginnings.

5. Your Feelings Matter
No feeling is too big or too small. What you feel is important, and you deserve kindness, especially from yourself. Talk to yourself as you would to a friend who is feeling sad.

Positive Thoughts

6. Sadness Can Be A Teacher
Even though it is tough, sadness can help you understand yourself better. It can teach you what truly matters to you and remind you to take care of your heart.

7. Memories Can Be A Warm Blanket
Think of a time when you felt safe, happy, or loved. Hold onto that feeling, like wrapping yourself in a warm blanket. Good memories remind us that happiness is always within reach.

8. Breathe Through The Tough Moments
When sadness feels too heavy, take slow, deep breaths. Inhale calm, exhale worry. Each breath is a gentle reminder that you are here, and you are strong.

9. Kindness Can Light The Way
Even when you feel down, a small act of kindness, toward yourself or someone else, can bring light into your day. Gentle laughter, a kind word, or a lovely thought can shift your energy.

10. This Feeling Will Not Last Forever
It may seem like sadness will never go away, but just like night turns into day, emotions change. You are stronger than this moment, and brighter days are ahead.

Affirmations

1. I am allowed to feel my emotions, but they do not define me.
2. I am loved and cared for, even when I feel alone.
3. Small joys are all around me, even on hard days.
4. My feelings matter, and I give myself kindness.
5. I can find moments of peace, even in sadness.
6. I am strong enough to get through this.
7. It's okay to take my time to heal and feel better.
8. I am not my sadness; I am so much more.
9. I trust that happiness will return to me.
10. I deserve love, comfort, and brighter days ahead.

Interactive Reflections

Journaling Prompt:
What is one thing that made you feel peaceful, even a little, today? Write about it, even if it was something small.

Friend Connection:
Think of a friend who might be feeling sad. How can you reach out to them? Write down one way you can show them you care.

Interactive Reflections

Reflection Questions:
What did you learn about sadness from this chapter?
How can you remind yourself of the small joys in your life when you are feeling down?

Weekly Challenge:
This week, try to find one small joy every day, whether it is a nice memory, a kind word, or something you enjoy doing. Keep a journal of these moments.

Activity Page

Think of three things that bring you comfort when you are feeling down. It could be some music you like, a wonderful memory, or a hug from someone you love. Write them down and keep them close for when you need something to cheer you up and make you joyful once

YOUR OWN AFFIRMATION

Write Your Own Affirmations

Write Something Kind About Yourself

Ask My Heart

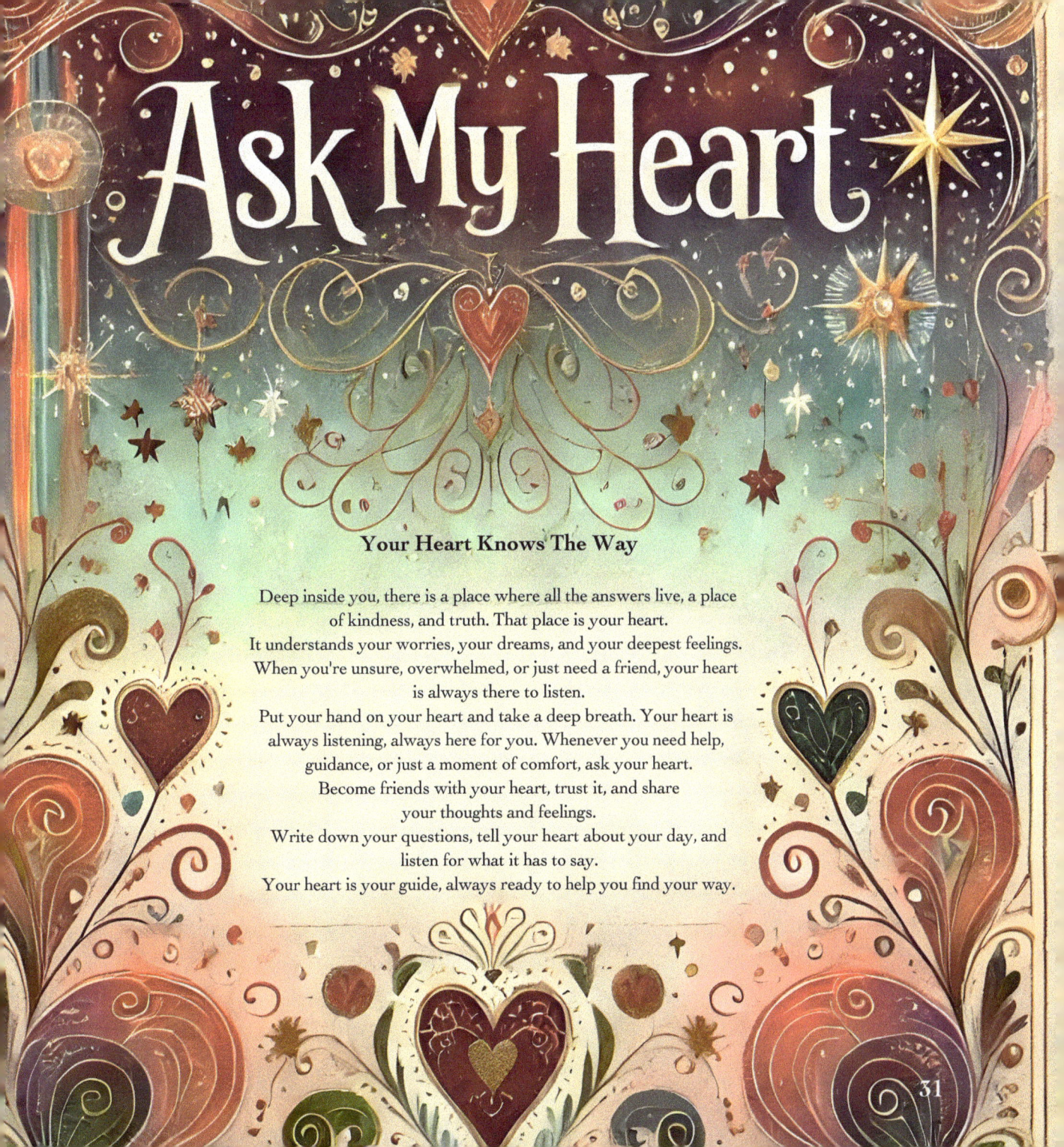

Your Heart Knows The Way

Deep inside you, there is a place where all the answers live, a place of kindness, and truth. That place is your heart.
It understands your worries, your dreams, and your deepest feelings. When you're unsure, overwhelmed, or just need a friend, your heart is always there to listen.
Put your hand on your heart and take a deep breath. Your heart is always listening, always here for you. Whenever you need help, guidance, or just a moment of comfort, ask your heart.
Become friends with your heart, trust it, and share your thoughts and feelings.
Write down your questions, tell your heart about your day, and listen for what it has to say.
Your heart is your guide, always ready to help you find your way.

BEDTIME THOUGHTS

For Relaxation & Calm

Gentle Reflection & Gratitude
Before you sleep, think of one thing that made you smile today. It could be something funny, kind, or a new discovery. Hold onto that happy thought as you rest.

Comforting Words
You are safe. You are cared for. Tomorrow is a fresh start, full of new adventures. Let go of any worries and rest peacefully.

Positive Affirmations
"I am brave. I am kind. I am loved. Everything is okay." (Whisper this to yourself before sleep.)

BEDTIME THOUGHTS

For Relaxation & Calm

My Prayers
Take a moment to connect with Grace and Love. Whether you believe in God, Angels, or a Divine power, know that you are lovingly watched over. Offer your prayers and feel the peace that comes from being heard and supported.

Simple Breathing Exercise
Breathe in slowly through your nose, then exhale gently through your mouth. Imagine your breath as a soft wave, washing away the day. With each breath, feel the peace.

A Short Visualisation
Close your eyes and picture yourself in a warm, cozy place a soft cloud, a glowing meadow, or a magical treehouse. Feel safe, calm, and ready for sleep.

Thoughts & Reflections

My Dear Heart

You are always with me, always listening, always knowing what I need. You hold my dreams, my worries, my joys, and my questions. When I feel lost, you help me find my way. When I am unsure, you remind me of what truly matters.

I will learn to listen to you, to trust you, and to ask for your guidance. You are my friend, my safe place, my quiet strength.

Now, I will take a deep breath, put my hand on my heart, and ask, what do you want to tell me today?

Write your thoughts here or on a piece of paper.

My Dear Heart

My Notes

CHAPTER 2
CALM IN THE STORM

(For When You Are Feeling Worried Or Anxious)

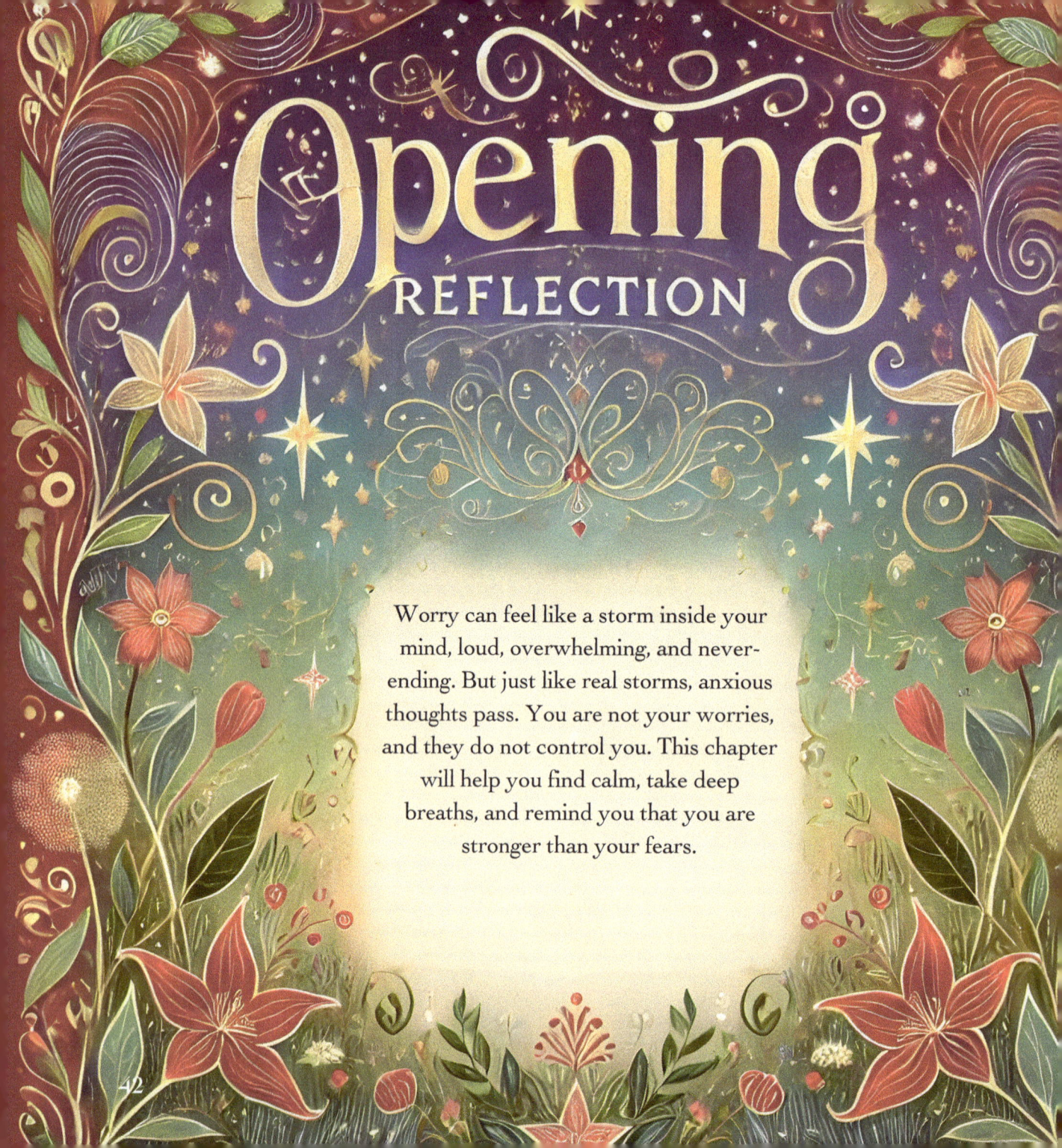

Opening Reflection

Worry can feel like a storm inside your mind, loud, overwhelming, and never-ending. But just like real storms, anxious thoughts pass. You are not your worries, and they do not control you. This chapter will help you find calm, take deep breaths, and remind you that you are stronger than your fears.

Emotion Wheel Activity

Now, take a moment to look at the section of the Emotion Wheel that represents how you feel right now. This can help you connect with your emotions and express them.

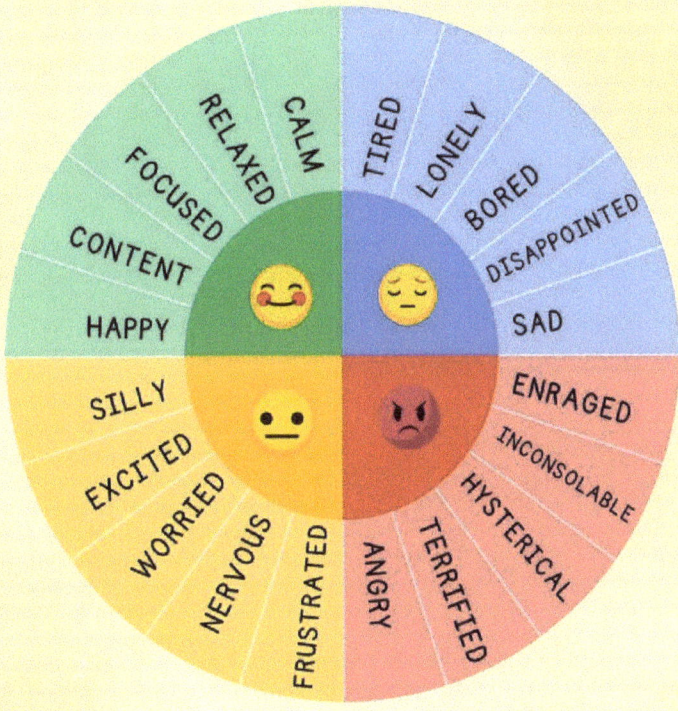

Positive Reminder:

Remember, worry is just a feeling, and it does not have to control you. You have the power to find calm within the storm.

How Do I Feel Today?

Take a moment to check in with yourself and write down how you are feeling right now? It is okay to feel a mix of emotions; whatever you're feeling is valid.

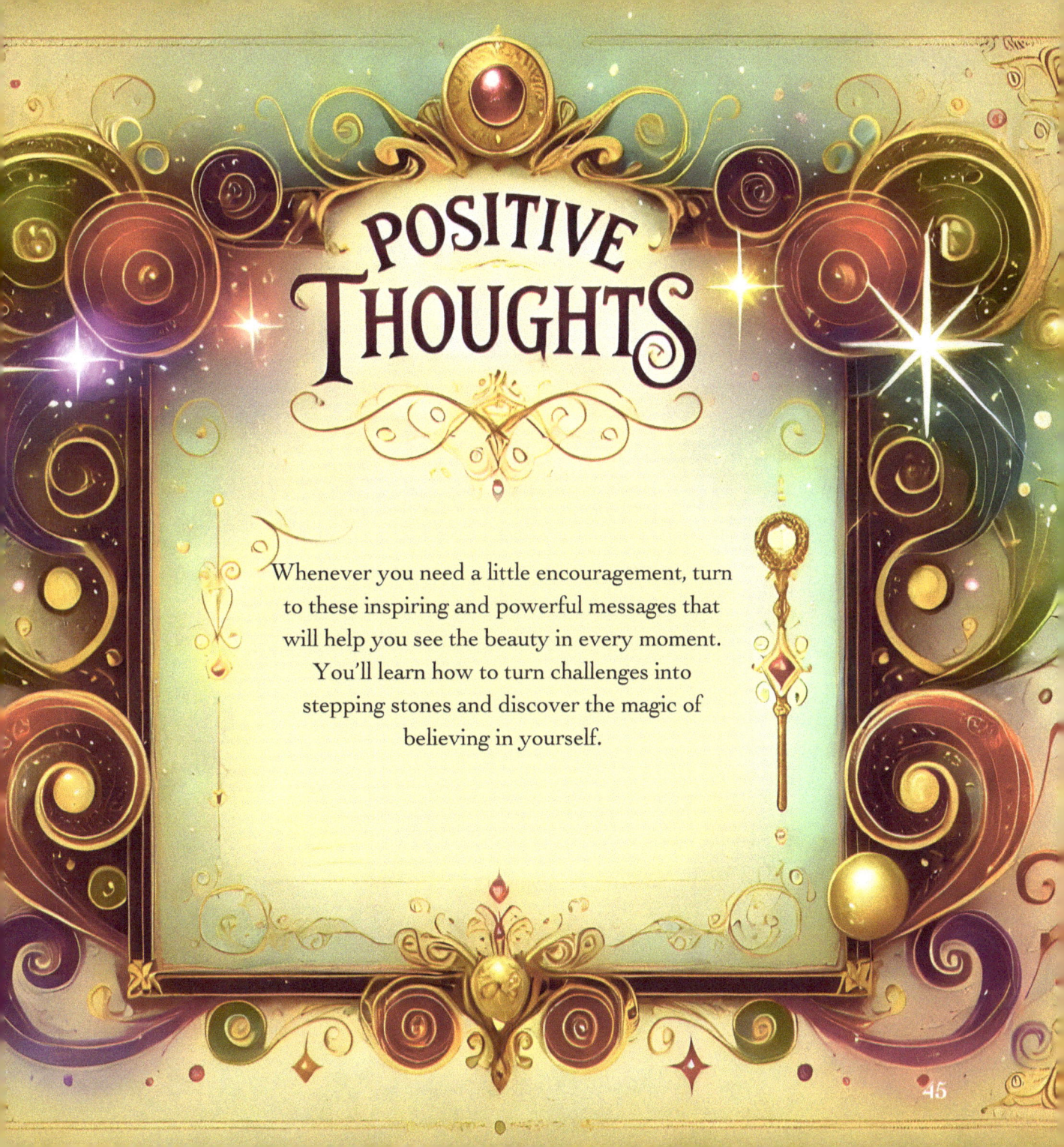

POSITIVE THOUGHTS

Whenever you need a little encouragement, turn to these inspiring and powerful messages that will help you see the beauty in every moment. You'll learn how to turn challenges into stepping stones and discover the magic of believing in yourself.

Positive Thoughts

1. Your Thoughts Are Like Clouds
Worries may fill your mind like dark clouds in the sky, but they do not stay forever. Let them drift by without holding onto them. Soon, the sky will clear.

2. You Are Safe Right Now
Anxiety often makes you think about "what ifs." But in this moment, you are here, and you are safe. Focusing on the present can help ease your worries.

3. Breathe, and Let It Go
When your mind feels overwhelmed, take slow, deep breaths. Each inhale fills you with calm, and each exhale releases tension.

4. Not Every Thought Is True
Just because a thought enters your mind does not mean it's real or will happen. You have the power to question your worries and remind yourself of the truth.

5. You Are More Than Your Worries
Anxious thoughts do not define you. You are strong, capable, and able to handle whatever comes your way.

Positive Thoughts

6. Small Steps Can Make A Big Difference
When something feels too big to handle, break it into tiny steps. Focus on just the next step, and then the next. You do not have to do everything at once.

7. Your Feelings Are Temporary
No feeling lasts forever, not even worry. Just as waves rise and fall, your emotions will settle. Trust that this feeling will pass.

8. A Peaceful Place Is Within You
Imagine a place where you feel safe and calm. It could be a beach, a woods, or a sunny garden. Close your eyes and picture yourself there whenever you need comfort.

9. Your Body Can Help You Feel Better
Stretch, take a walk, drink some water; small actions can tell your body that everything is okay. Movement can help quiet a racing mind.

10. You Have Faced Worry Before and Overcome It
Think of a time when you felt worried, but everything turned out fine. You have faced challenges before, and you made it through. You will this time, too.

AFFIRMATIONS

1. I am safe, and I can handle this moment.
2. My thoughts do not control me.
3. Each deep breath brings me calm and peace.
4. I am stronger than my worries.
5. I do not have to figure everything out right now.
6. I choose to focus on what I can control and let go of what I can't.
7. I trust that this feeling will pass.
8. My body is relaxed, and my mind is at ease.
9. With courage I am capable of handling anything.
10. I allow myself to find peace in this moment.

Interactive Reflections

Journaling Prompt:
Write down three things that help you feel calm. It could be a favourite meal, a beloved pet, or a hobby you enjoy. Keep this list handy for when you need it.

Friend Connection:
If you notice a friend looking anxious, how can you help them feel calm? Write down one thing you could do together.

Interactive Reflections

Reflection Questions:
What ideas that you've read in this chapter, can you apply when you feel anxious?

How can you remind yourself that your worries are not permanent?

Weekly Challenge:
Choose one calming activity each day this week, such as deep breathing or a short walk, and note how it helps you feel more at ease.

ACTIVITY PAGE

Try the 5-4-3-2-1 Grounding Technique when you are feeling anxious:

- Name 5 things you can see.
- Name 4 things you can touch.
- Name 3 things you can hear.
- Name 2 things you can smell.
- Name 1 thing you love about yourself.

YOUR OWN AFFIRMATION

Write Your Own Affirmations

WRITE Something Kind ABOUT YOURSELF

Ask My Heart

Your Heart Knows The Way

Deep inside you, there is a place where all the answers live, a place of kindness, and truth. That place is your heart.
It understands your worries, your dreams, and your deepest feelings. When you're unsure, overwhelmed, or just need a friend, your heart is always there to listen.
Put your hand on your heart and take a deep breath. Your heart is always listening, always here for you. Whenever you need help, guidance, or just a moment of comfort, ask your heart.
Become friends with your heart, trust it, and share your thoughts and feelings.
Write down your questions, tell your heart about your day, and listen for what it has to say.
Your heart is your guide, always ready to help you find your way.

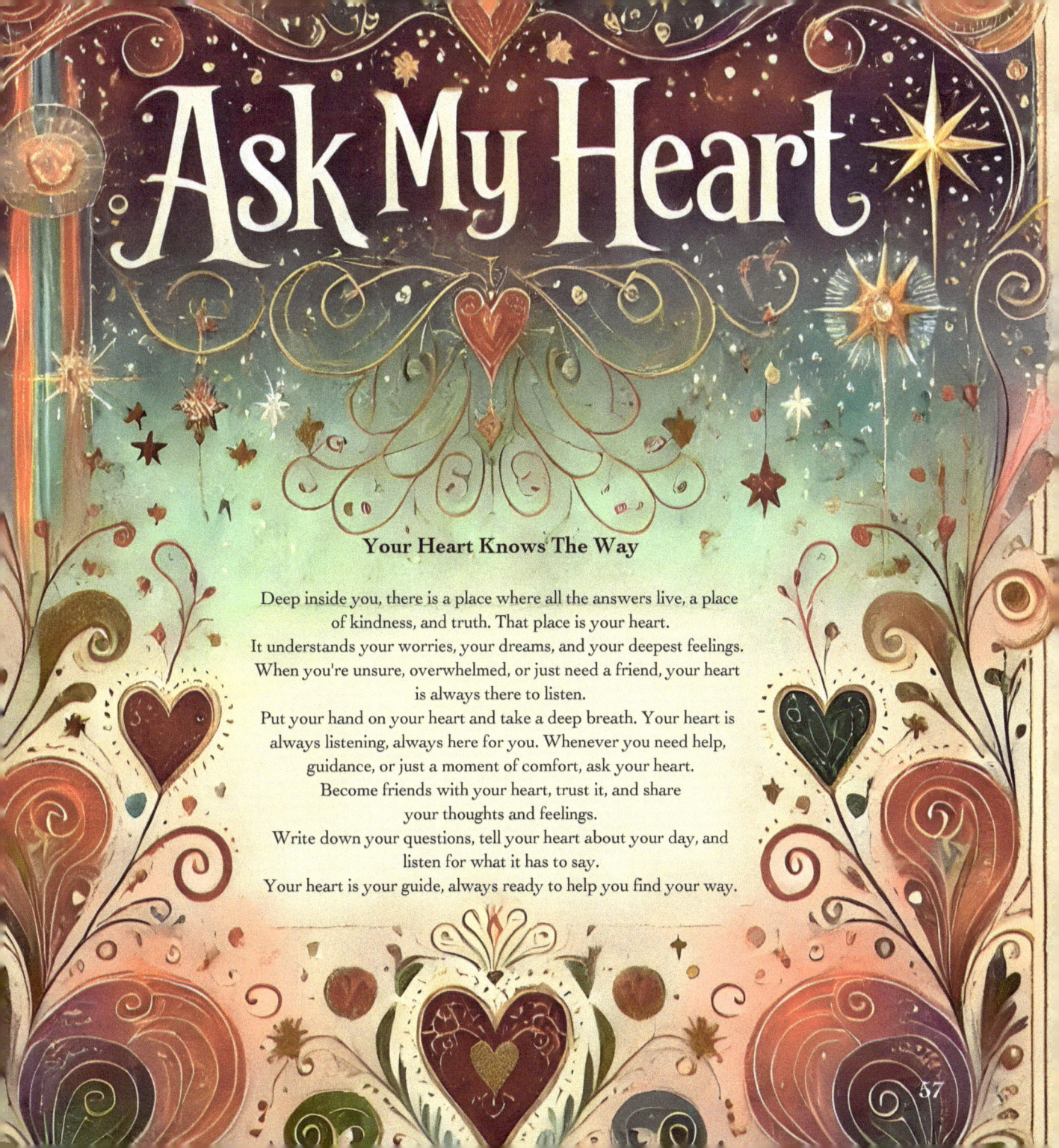

BEDTIME THOUGHTS

For Relaxation & Calm

Gentle Reflection & Gratitude
Think of someone who made your day better. Maybe they made you laugh, offered kind words, or lent a hand. Send them a silent thank-you as you settle down for the night.

Comforting Words
You are important. You matter. Everything you did today was enough. Tomorrow is a new beginning, so rest knowing you are loved just as you are.

Positive Affirmations
"I am strong. I am peaceful. I am enough."

BEDTIME THOUGHTS

For Relaxation & Calm

My Prayers
Take a moment to connect with Grace and Love. Whether you believe in God, Angels, or a Divine power, know that you are lovingly watched over. Offer your prayers and feel the peace that comes from being heard and supported.

A Simple Breathing Exercise
Take a deep breath in, then let it out slowly, like blowing out a candle. With each breath, feel yourself becoming lighter and more relaxed.

A Short Visualisation
Imagine you are gently floating on a quiet river. The stars above watch over you as you drift into a peaceful sleep.

My Dear Heart

You are always with me, always listening, always knowing what I need. You hold my dreams, my worries, my joys, and my questions. When I feel lost, you help me find my way. When I am unsure, you remind me of what truly matters.

I will learn to listen to you, to trust you, and to ask for your guidance. You are my friend, my safe place, my quiet strength.

Now, I will take a deep breath, put my hand on my heart, and ask, what do you want to tell me today?

Write your thoughts here or on a piece of paper.

My Dear Heart

CHAPTER 3
BRAVE AND STRONG

(For When You Are Feeling Scared)

Opening REFLECTION

Fear is a natural feeling, but it does not have to control you. Just like a small candle can light up a dark room, even the tiniest bit of courage can make fear feel smaller. You have faced challenges before, and you have the strength to face this one too. This is a reminder for you that bravery is not about never feeling afraid; it is about taking a step forward, even when you are.

Emotion Wheel Activity

Now, take a moment to look at the section of the Emotion Wheel that represents how you feel right now. This can help you connect with your emotions and express them.

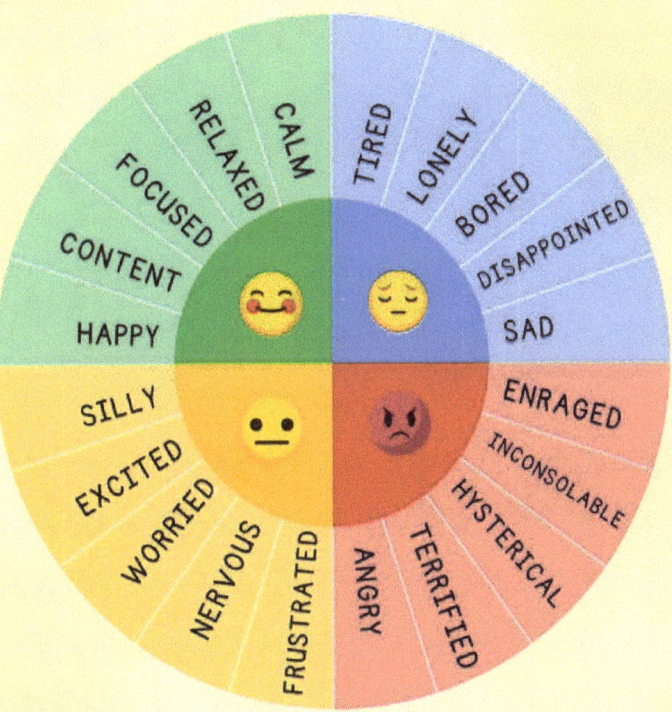

Positive Reminder:

Remember, fear is a natural feeling, and it does not have to stop you. You have the courage to face whatever comes your way.

How Do I Feel Today?

Take a moment to check in with yourself and write down how you are feeling right now? It is okay to feel a mix of emotions; whatever you're feeling is valid.

POSITIVE THOUGHTS

Whenever you need a little encouragement, turn to these inspiring and powerful messages that will help you see the beauty in every moment. You'll learn how to turn challenges into stepping stones and discover the magic of believing in yourself.

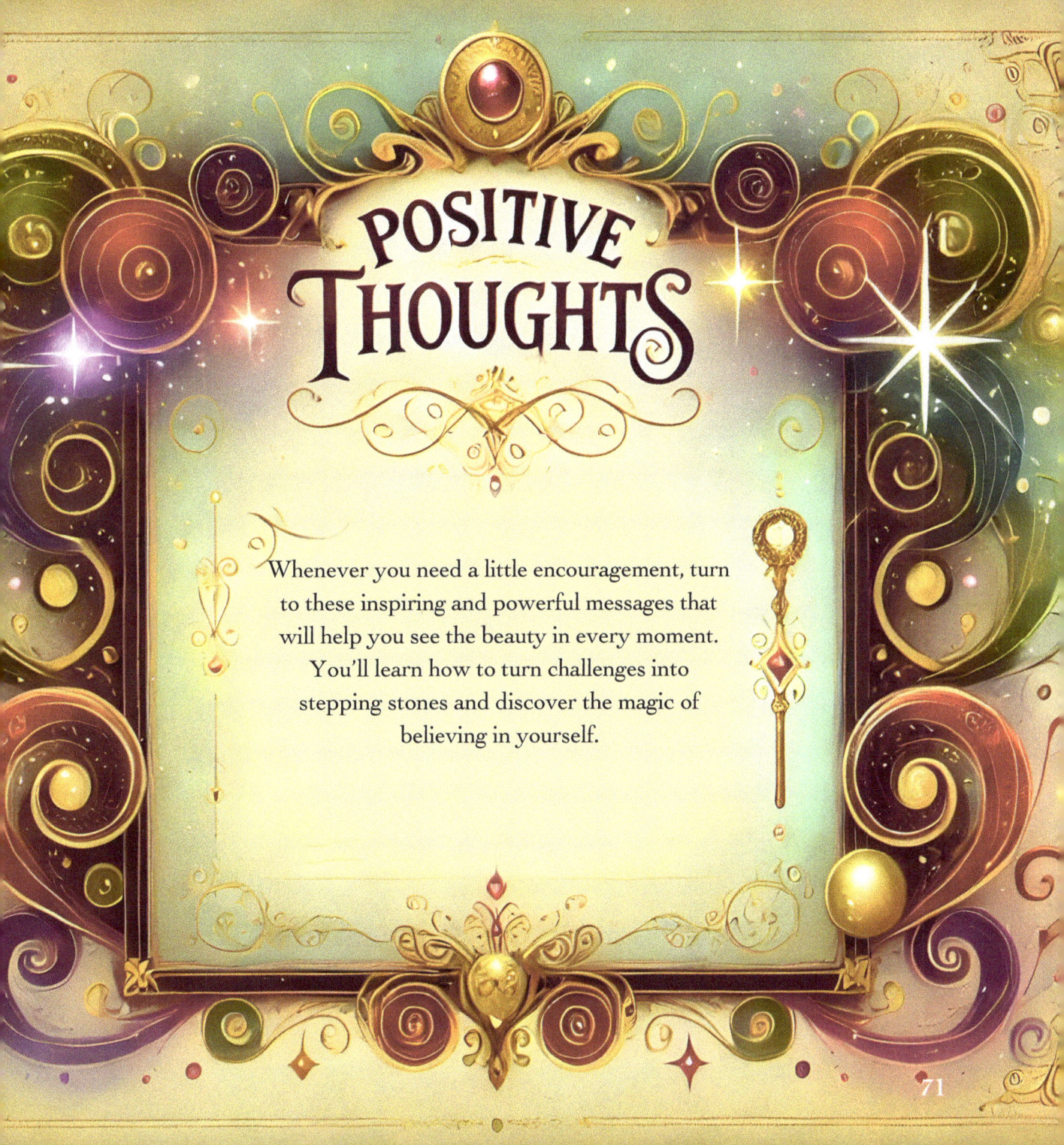

Positive Thoughts

1. Fear Is Just A Feeling
Fear might feel big, but it is just an emotion; it cannot stop you. You have the power to move through it and come out stronger.

2. Bravery Is Not The Absence Of Fear
Courage does not mean you are never scared. It means you feel the fear but take action anyway. You are braver than you think.

3. You Have Done Hard Things Before
Think of a time when you felt afraid but still moved forward. You made it through. This time is no different.

4. Fear Exaggerates The Truth
Fear tells us stories that are not always true. Ask yourself: Is this fear real, or is it just my mind playing tricks on me?

5. You Are Never Alone
When fear makes you feel lonely, just remember that there are people around you who care and want to help. Think about the amazing world we live in, with all the stars in the sky, the big oceans, and the tall mountains. There is a special power behind it all, known as God, who created everything, including you! You are loved and never truly alone, no matter how tough things may seem.

Positive Thoughts

6. Every Small Step Is A Victory
You do not have to be fearless all at once. Each step forward, no matter how small, is proof of your courage.

7. Fear Can Be A Teacher
Sometimes, fear is a sign that you are growing and stepping into something new. Instead of running from it, ask what it's teaching you.

8. Your Inner Strength Is Greater Than Any Fear
Inside you is a deep well of strength. No matter what happens, you have everything you need to handle it.

9. Fear Fades When You Face It
The more you avoid fear, the bigger it feels. But when you take even one brave step, fear starts to shrink.

10. You Are Braver Than You Know
Even if you don't feel it right now, courage is already inside you. Trust yourself; you've got this.

Affirmations

1. I am brave, even when I feel afraid.
2. I trust myself to handle any challenge.
3. Fear is just a feeling; it does not define me.
4. Every step I take makes me stronger.
5. I have overcome fear before, and I can do it again.
6. My courage grows every time I face my fears.
7. I am surrounded by love and support.
8. I believe in myself, even in uncertain moments.
9. I let go of fear and step into my strength.
10. I am safe, strong, and capable.

Interactive Reflections

Journaling Prompt:
Think of a time when you did something that scared you. How did you feel afterwards?

Friend Connection:
Think of a time when you were afraid. How did a friend help you? Write down how you can be there for a friend facing their fears.

Interactive Reflections

Reflection Questions:
What fears have you faced in the past, and how did you overcome them?

How can you remind yourself of your inner strength when fear arises?

Weekly Challenge:
This week, take one small step towards facing a fear. It could be as simple as speaking up for yourself or trying something new.

Activity Page

Write down one fear you have and then write three reasons why you are strong enough to face it.

Activity Page Answers

Answers

YOUR OWN AFFIRMATION

Write Your Own Affirmations

WRITE Something Kind ABOUT YOURSELF

Ask My Heart

Your Heart Knows The Way

Deep inside you, there is a place where all the answers live, a place
of kindness, and truth. That place is your heart.
It understands your worries, your dreams, and your deepest feelings.
When you're unsure, overwhelmed, or just need a friend, your heart
is always there to listen.
Put your hand on your heart and take a deep breath. Your heart is
always listening, always here for you. Whenever you need help,
guidance, or just a moment of comfort, ask your heart.
Become friends with your heart, trust it, and share
your thoughts and feelings.
Write down your questions, tell your heart about your day, and
listen for what it has to say.
Your heart is your guide, always ready to help you find your way.

BEDTIME THOUGHTS

For Relaxation & Calm

Gentle Reflection & Gratitude
Recall a moment today when you felt happy. Let that warm feeling fill your heart and ease you into a restful night.

Comforting Words
You are loved and cared for. You have done your best today. Release your worries and embrace the calm of the night.

Positive Affirmations
"I am kind. I am capable. I am growing every day."

BEDTIME THOUGHTS

For Relaxation & Calm

My Prayers
Take a moment to connect with Grace and Love. Whether you believe in God, Angels, or a Divine power, know that you are lovingly watched over. Offer your prayers and feel the peace that comes from being heard and supported.

Simple Breathing Exercise
Place one hand on your belly and one hand on your chest. Take a deep breath in for a count of four, then exhale slowly for a count of four. Repeat until you feel peaceful.

A Short Visualisation
Picture yourself in a beautiful field of flowers, bathed in soft moonlight. The gentle glow and twinkling stars leave you feeling completely safe and at ease.

Thoughts & Reflections

My Dear Heart

You are always with me, always listening, always knowing what I need. You hold my dreams, my worries, my joys, and my questions. When I feel lost, you help me find my way. When I am unsure, you remind me of what truly matters.

I will learn to listen to you, to trust you, and to ask for your guidance. You are my friend, my safe place, my quiet strength.

Now, I will take a deep breath, put my hand on my heart, and ask, what do you want to tell me today?

Write your thoughts here or on a piece of paper.

My Dear Heart

My Notes

CHAPTER 4
YOU ARE ENOUGH

(For When You Are Feeling Insecure Or Not Good Enough)

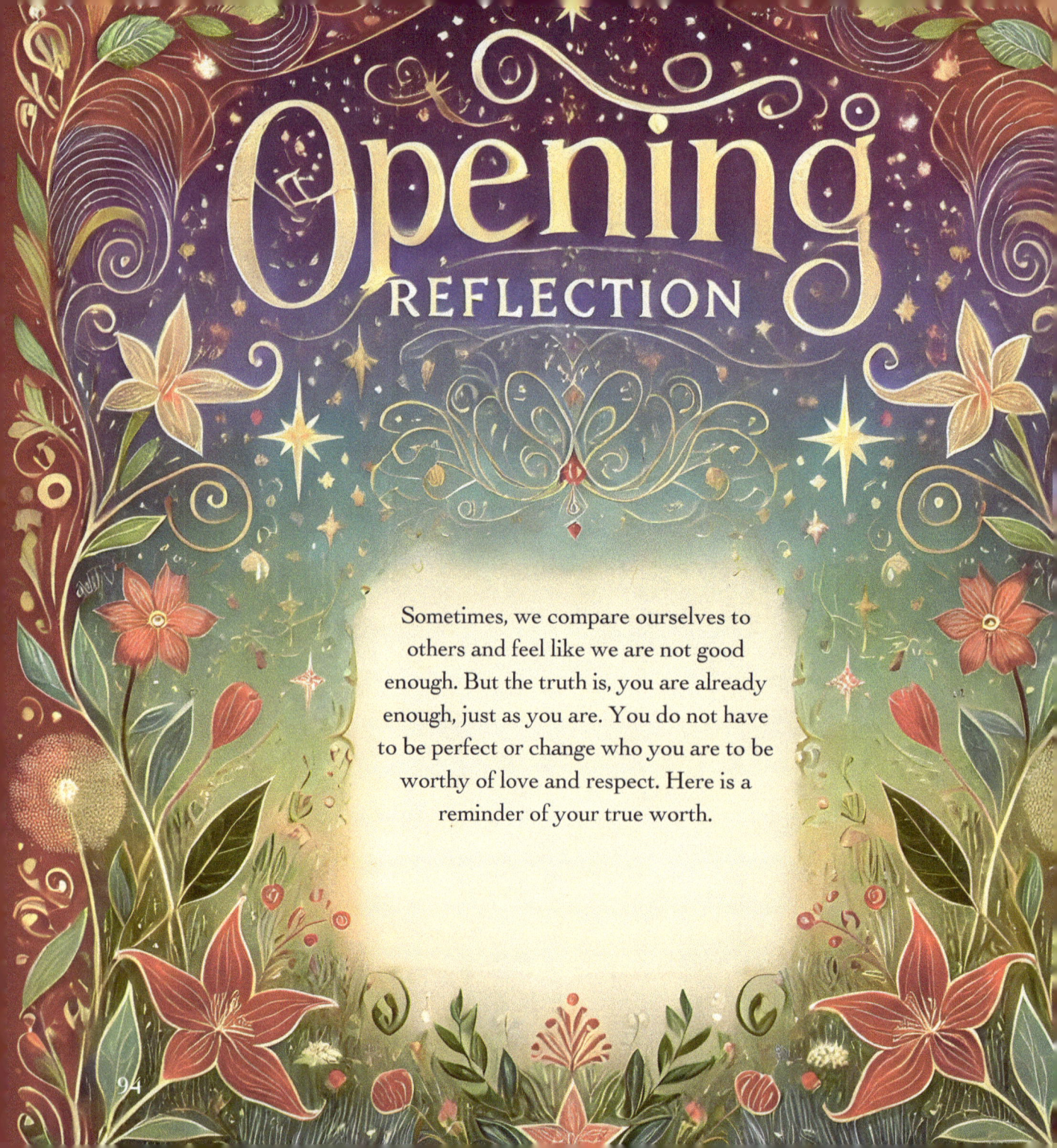

Opening
REFLECTION

Sometimes, we compare ourselves to others and feel like we are not good enough. But the truth is, you are already enough, just as you are. You do not have to be perfect or change who you are to be worthy of love and respect. Here is a reminder of your true worth.

Emotion Wheel Activity

Now, take a moment to look at the section of the Emotion Wheel that represents how you feel right now. This can help you connect with your emotions and express them.

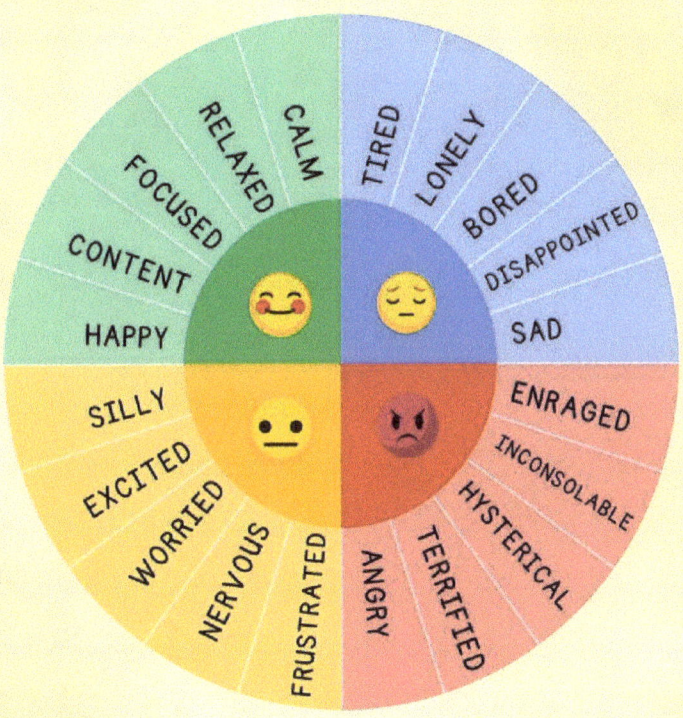

Positive Reminder:

Remember, you are enough just as you are. You do not need to change to be worthy of love and respect.

How Do I Feel Today?

Take a moment to check in with yourself and write down how you are feeling right now? It is okay to feel a mix of emotions; whatever you're feeling is valid.

POSITIVE THOUGHTS

Whenever you need a little encouragement, turn to these inspiring and powerful messages that will help you see the beauty in every moment. You'll learn how to turn challenges into stepping stones and discover the magic of believing in yourself.

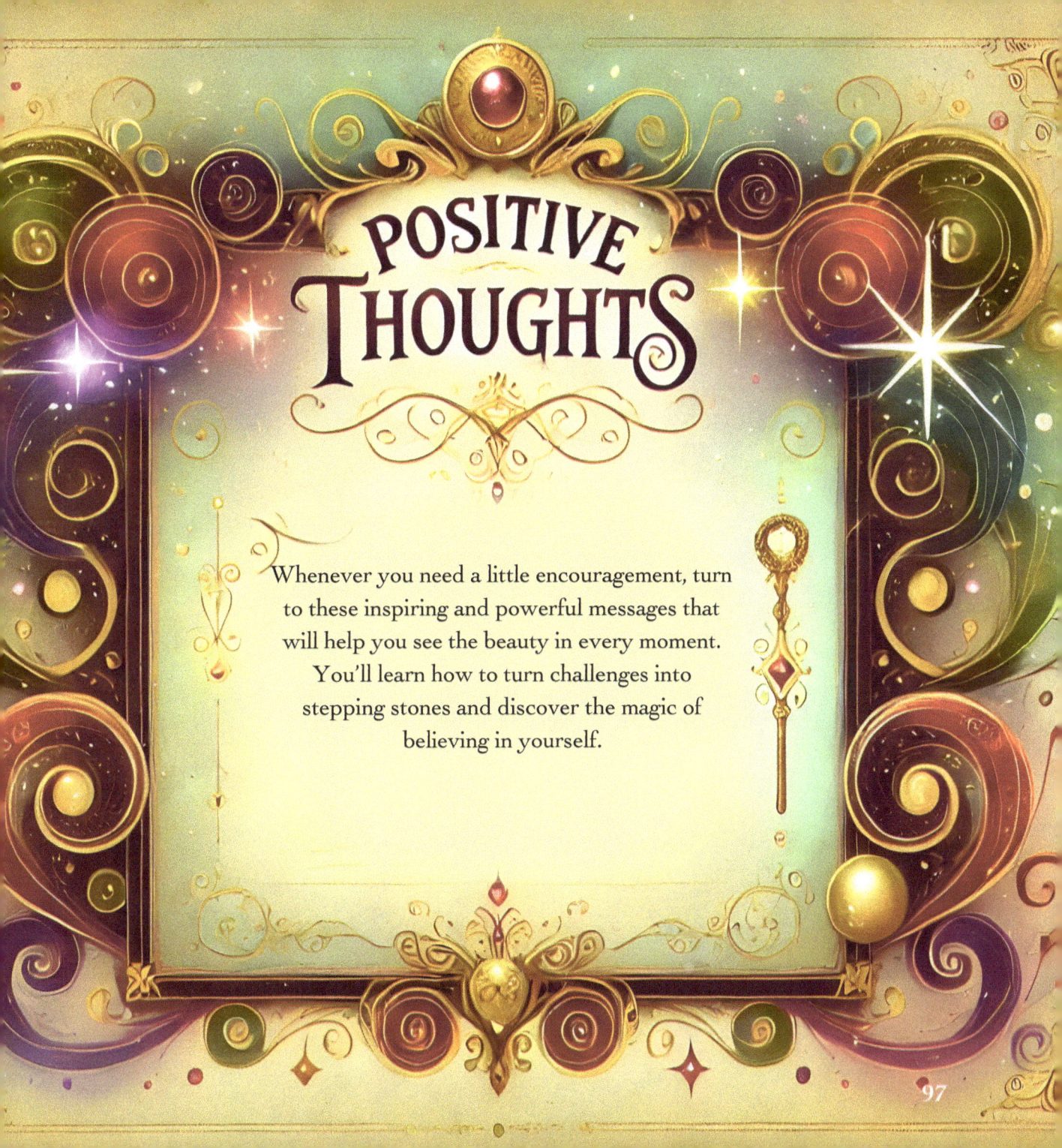

Positive Thoughts

1. You Do Not Have To Be Perfect
Perfection is impossible. You are wonderful just as you are, flaws and all.

2. Comparison Is A Trick
It is easy to look at others and feel like you are not enough. But no one sees the full story; you are special in your own way.

3. You Have Unique Gifts
There is no one else exactly like you. Your thoughts, kindness, and talents make the world a better place.

4. Your Worth Is Not Measured By Achievements
You do not have to accomplish something to be valuable. You matter simply because you exist.

5. Self-Love Is A Superpower
The more you believe in yourself, the stronger you become. Treat yourself with kindness; you deserve it.

Positive Thoughts

6. You Are More Than What Others Think
People's opinions do not change your worth. Only you get to decide how you see yourself.

7. Mistakes Do Not Define You
Everyone makes mistakes. They don't make you less; they help you grow.

8. You Are Loved As You Are
You do not have to change to be loved. You are already enough for the right people.

9. Your Feelings Are Valid
It is okay to feel insecure sometimes, but do not let those feelings make you forget how amazing you are.

10. You Shine In Your Own Way
Like stars in the sky, everyone shines differently. Your light is just as important as anyone else's.

AFFIRMATIONS

1. I am enough, just as I am.
2. I do not need to compare myself to anyone else.
3. My worth is not measured by what I do, but by who I am.
4. I am unique, and that is my strength.
5. I am proud of who I am becoming.
6. I deserve love and kindness.
7. Mistakes do not define me; they help me grow.
8. I choose to see myself with kindness and love.
9. My voice, my thoughts, and my heart matter.
10. I am worthy, always.

Interactive Reflections

Journaling Prompt:
What makes you special? Think about your kindness, the way you care for others, or something that makes you proud.

Friend Connection:
Encourage a friend by reminding them of their strengths. Write down a compliment you can share with them.

Interactive Reflections

Reflection Questions:
What is one thing you love about yourself?

How can you practice self-love every day?

Weekly Challenge:
This week, practice one act of self-kindness each day. It could be treating yourself to something nice or taking time to relax.

Activity Page

Write down five things you like about yourself.
They can be big or small.

Activity Page Answers

YOUR OWN AFFIRMATION

Write Your Own Affirmations

Write Something Kind About Yourself

Ask My Heart

Your Heart Knows The Way

Deep inside you, there is a place where all the answers live, a place of kindness, and truth. That place is your heart.
It understands your worries, your dreams, and your deepest feelings. When you're unsure, overwhelmed, or just need a friend, your heart is always there to listen.
Put your hand on your heart and take a deep breath. Your heart is always listening, always here for you. Whenever you need help, guidance, or just a moment of comfort, ask your heart.
Become friends with your heart, trust it, and share your thoughts and feelings.
Write down your questions, tell your heart about your day, and listen for what it has to say.
Your heart is your guide, always ready to help you find your way.

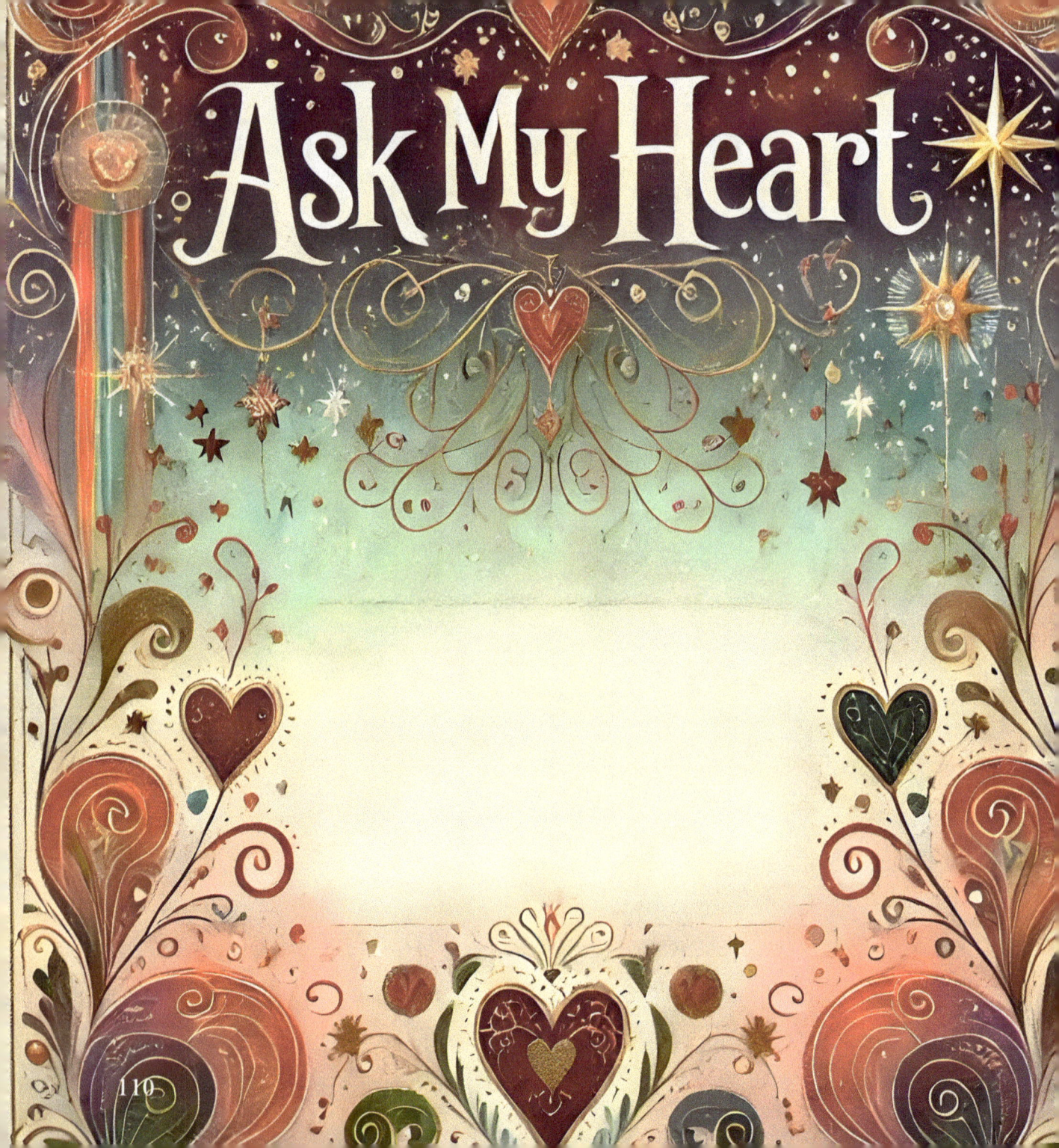

BEDTIME THOUGHTS

For Relaxation & Calm

Gentle Reflection & Gratitude
Think of one thing you accomplished today, big or small. Celebrate that achievement, whether you learned something new, helped someone, or simply tried your best.

Comforting Words
You are exactly where you need to be. You don't need all the answers right now. Rest, and let tomorrow bring new light.

Positive Affirmations
"I am learning. I am growing. I am doing my best."

BEDTIME THOUGHTS

For Relaxation & Calm

My Prayers
Take a moment to connect with Grace and Love. Whether you believe in God, Angels, or a Divine power, know that you are lovingly watched over. Offer your prayers and feel the peace that comes from being heard and supported.

Simple Breathing Exercise
Close your eyes and take a deep breath in through your nose and hold your breath for a count of three. Exhale slowly through your mouth imagining all your tension leaving.

A Short Visualisation
Visualise a warm, glowing campfire. Watch the dancing flames and feel the comforting warmth as the quiet night stars shine on you, giving you the feeling of safety and peace.

My Dear Heart

You are always with me, always listening, always knowing what I need. You hold my dreams, my worries, my joys, and my questions. When I feel lost, you help me find my way. When I am unsure, you remind me of what truly matters.

I will learn to listen to you, to trust you, and to ask for your guidance. You are my friend, my safe place, my quiet strength.

Now, I will take a deep breath, put my hand on my heart, and ask, what do you want to tell me today?

Write your thoughts here or on a piece of paper.

My Dear Heart

My Notes

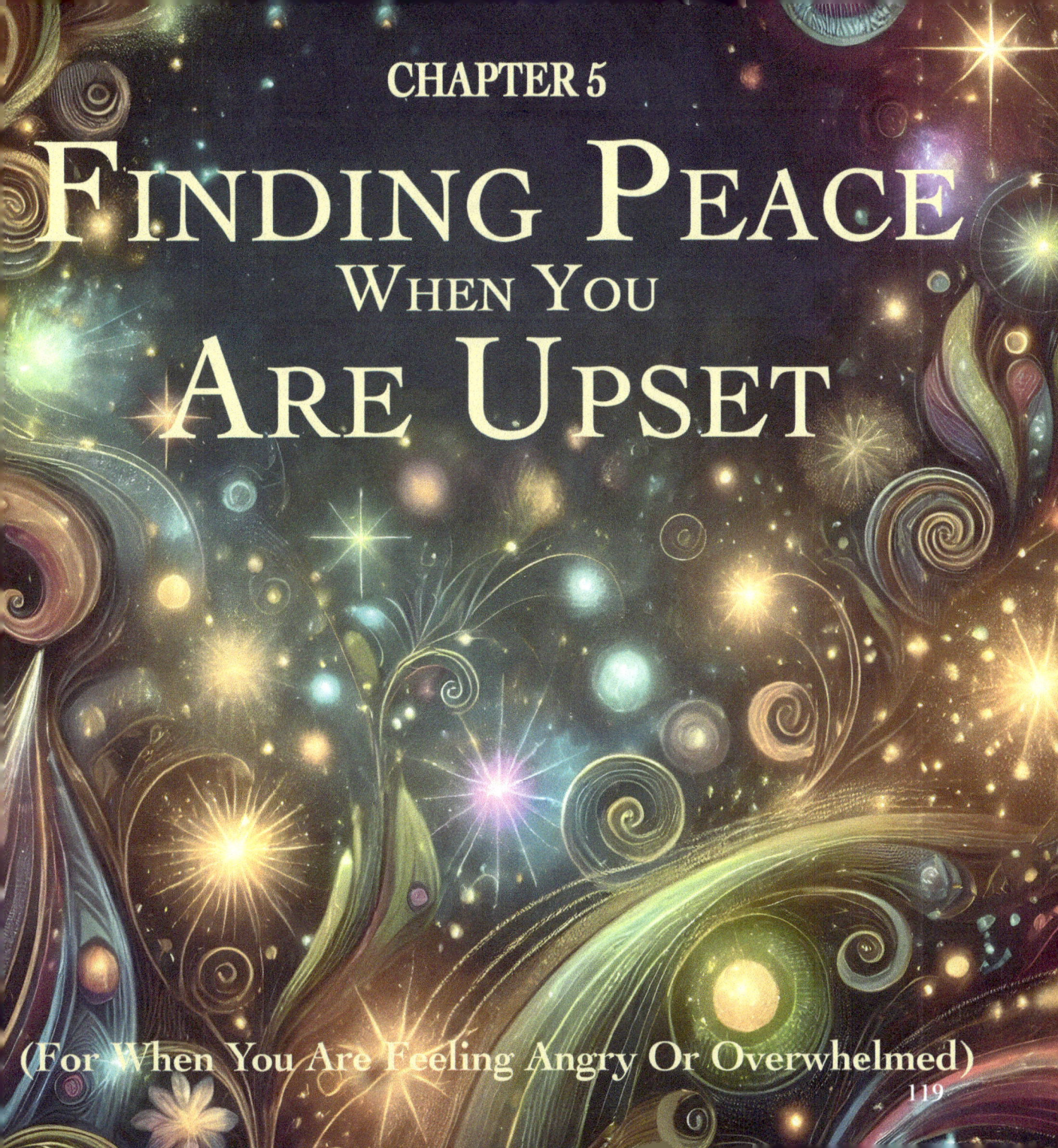

CHAPTER 5
Finding Peace When You Are Upset

(For When You Are Feeling Angry Or Overwhelmed)

Opening Reflection

Anger can feel like heat burning inside. Sometimes, it happens when things don't go our way. Other times, it comes from feeling hurt or misunderstood. Anger itself is not bad; it is what we do with it that matters. This chapter will help you find ways to calm the heat within and turn anger into understanding.

Emotion Wheel Activity

Now, take a moment to look at the section of the Emotion Wheel that represents how you feel right now. This can help you connect with your emotions and express them.

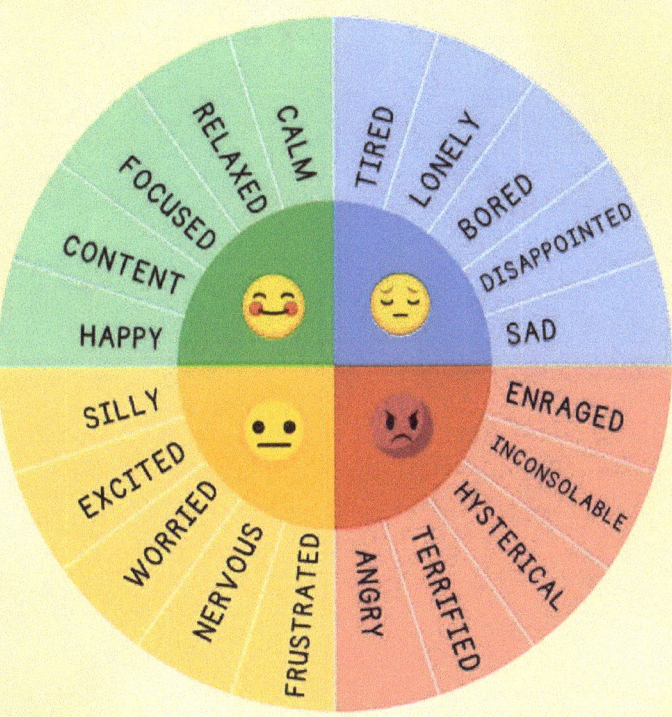

Positive Reminder:

Remember, anger is a natural emotion, and it can be managed. You have the power to find peace within yourself.

How Do I Feel Today?

Take a moment to check in with yourself and write down how you are feeling right now? It is okay to feel a mix of emotions; whatever you're feeling is valid.

POSITIVE THOUGHTS

Whenever you need a little encouragement, turn to these inspiring and powerful messages that will help you see the beauty in every moment. You'll learn how to turn challenges into stepping stones and discover the magic of believing in yourself.

Positive Thoughts

1. Anger Is A Natural Emotion
Feeling angry does not make you a bad person. It's just a signal that something needs your attention.

2. You Are In Control
Anger can feel powerful, but you are stronger. You always have the choice of how to respond.

3. Taking A Pause Can Help
Before reacting, take a deep breath. Give yourself a moment to think before you act.

4. Anger Often Hides Other Feelings
Sometimes, anger is covering up sadness, fear, or frustration. Ask yourself, "What am I really feeling?"

5. You Can Express Anger In A Healthy Way
Shouting or hurting others does not help, but talking, writing, or moving your body can release frustration in a positive way.

Positive Thoughts

6. Deep Breathing Can Calm The Storm
Breathe in for four seconds, hold it, then breathe out slowly. This helps your mind slow down.

7. Walking Away Is Sometimes The Best Choice
If a situation is making you too upset, it is okay to step away and come back later.

8. Not Everything Needs A Reaction
You do not have to respond to everything that upsets you. Some things are better left alone.

9. Kindness Can Dissolve Anger
Anger shrinks when met with kindness. Try responding with patience instead of more frustration.

10. You Can Let Go
Holding onto anger hurts you more than anyone else. When you're ready, you can choose peace.

Affirmations

1. I acknowledge my anger, but I choose how to respond.
2. I am in control of my feelings.
3. I can express my anger in healthy ways.
4. Taking a moment to breathe helps me feel better.
5. I will focus on solutions, not just the problem.
6. I respond with kindness, even when I feel upset.
7. I walk away from situations that are too intense.
8. My feelings are valid, and I can let them go.
9. I choose peace over frustration.
10. I am learning to manage my emotions effectively.

Interactive Reflections

Journaling Prompt:
What strategies can you use when you feel overwhelmed? Write down your ideas.

Friend Connection:
If you see a friend who seems angry, what can you say to help them feel better? Write down a supportive message you can share.

Interactive Reflections

Reflection Questions:
What triggers your anger, and how can you handle it differently next time?

How can you practice kindness toward yourself when you are feeling upset?

Weekly Challenge:
This week, every time you feel anger rising, pause and take three deep breaths. Then, write down your feelings and how you chose to respond.

Activity Page

Write down a situation that made you angry and think of a healthy way to express that anger if you ever feel that way again.

Write Something Kind About Yourself

Ask My Heart

Your Heart Knows The Way

Deep inside you, there is a place where all the answers live, a place of kindness, and truth. That place is your heart.
It understands your worries, your dreams, and your deepest feelings. When you're unsure, overwhelmed, or just need a friend, your heart is always there to listen.
Put your hand on your heart and take a deep breath. Your heart is always listening, always here for you. Whenever you need help, guidance, or just a moment of comfort, ask your heart.
Become friends with your heart, trust it, and share your thoughts and feelings.
Write down your questions, tell your heart about your day, and listen for what it has to say.
Your heart is your guide, always ready to help you find your way.

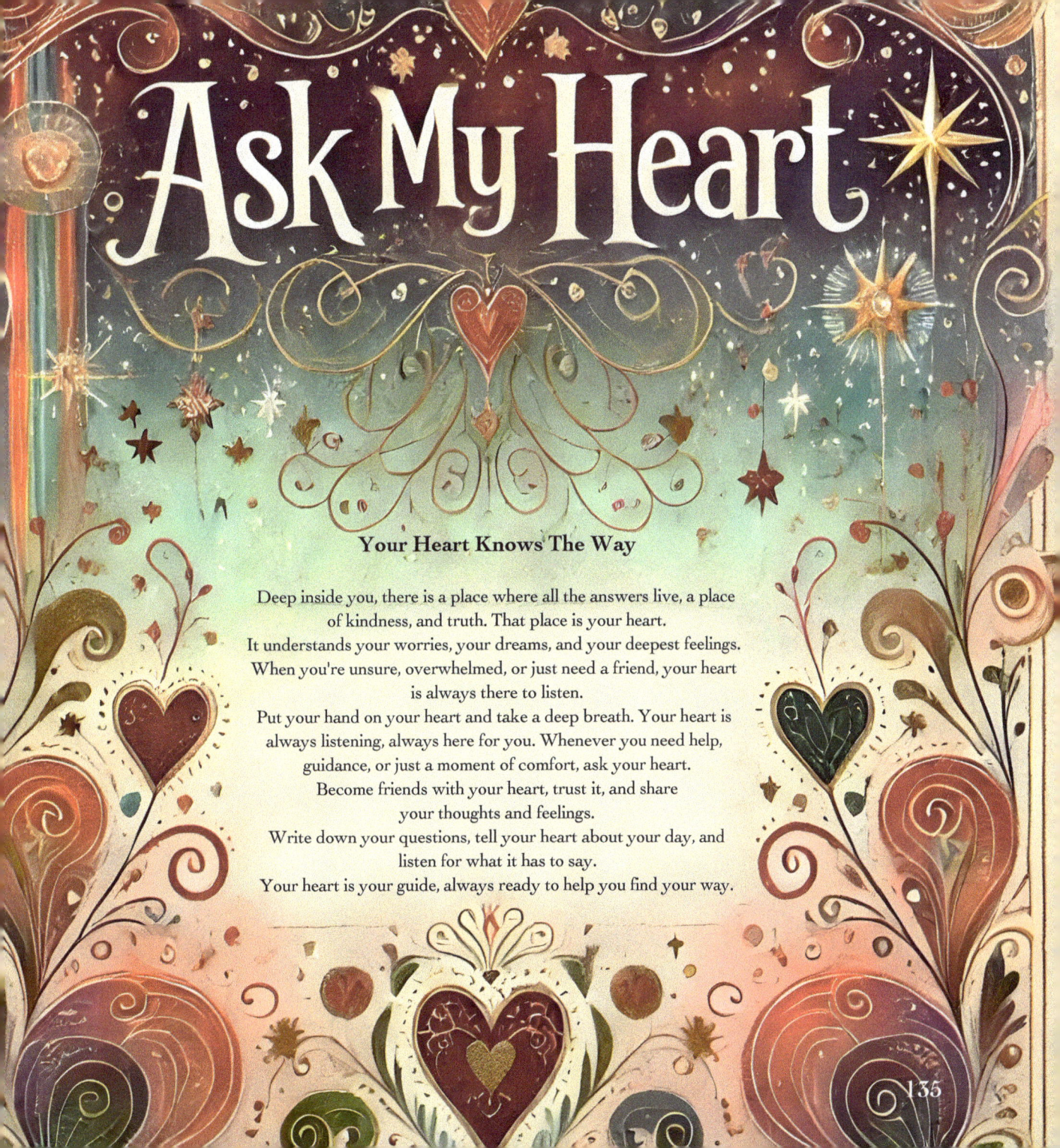

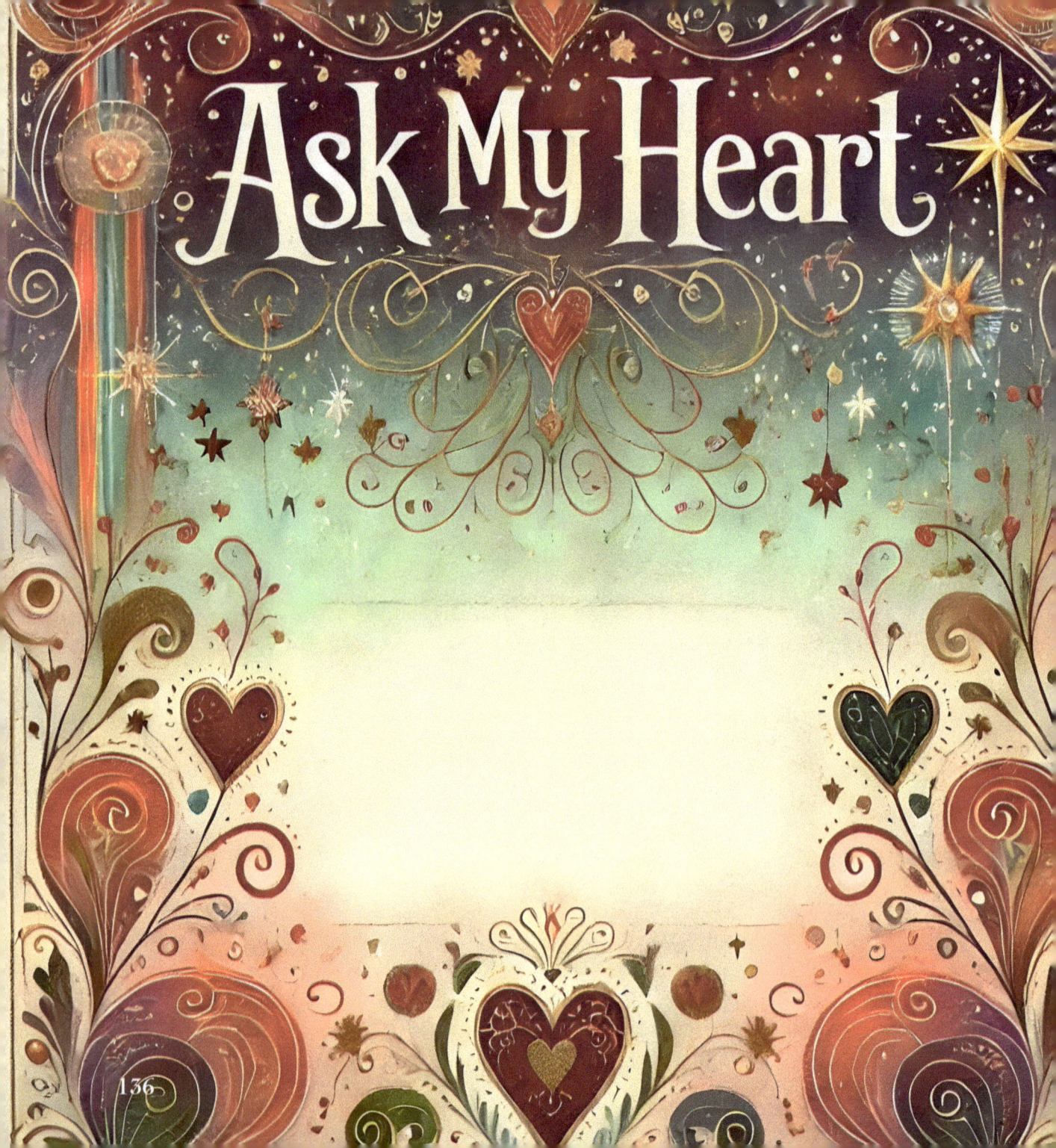

BEDTIME THOUGHTS

For Relaxation & Calm

Gentle Reflection & Gratitude
Think about a moment today when you felt challenged but chose to hold onto hope. Remember that even in tough times, hope is a guiding light. Celebrate yourself and your strength for not giving up, and let that spark of hope carry you into tomorrow with renewed courage.

Comforting Words
You are enough, just as you are. You don't need to be perfect. Embrace the love that surrounds you in this very moment.

Positive Affirmations
"I am calm. I am hopeful. I am loved."

BEDTIME THOUGHTS

For Relaxation & Calm

My Prayers
Take a moment to connect with Grace and Love. Whether you believe in God, Angels, or a Divine power, know that you are lovingly watched over. Offer your prayers and feel the peace that comes from being heard and supported.

Simple Breathing Exercise
Place one hand gently on your chest. As you take a deep in imagine your breath being a light filling your body, then exhale slowly releasing any worries.

A Short Visualisation
Close your eyes and feel the magic of your unique heartbeat, a rhythm that has existed before time and makes you a special spark.

My Dear Heart

You are always with me, always listening, always knowing what I need. You hold my dreams, my worries, my joys, and my questions. When I feel lost, you help me find my way. When I am unsure, you remind me of what truly matters.

I will learn to listen to you, to trust you, and to ask for your guidance. You are my friend, my safe place, my quiet strength.

Now, I will take a deep breath, put my hand on my heart, and ask, what do you want to tell me today?

Write your thoughts here or on a piece of paper.

My Dear Heart

My Notes

CHAPTER 6
A Heart Full Of Gratitude

(For When You Need To Focus On The Good)

Opening Reflection

Sometimes, it is easy to focus on what is missing or what's going wrong. But even on hard days, there are small moments of joy and kindness all around us. Gratitude is like a light; it helps us see the beauty in life, even when things aren't perfect. This chapter will help you shift your focus to what truly matters.

Emotion Wheel Activity

Now, take a moment to look at the section of the Emotion Wheel that represents how you feel right now. This can help you connect with your emotions and express them.

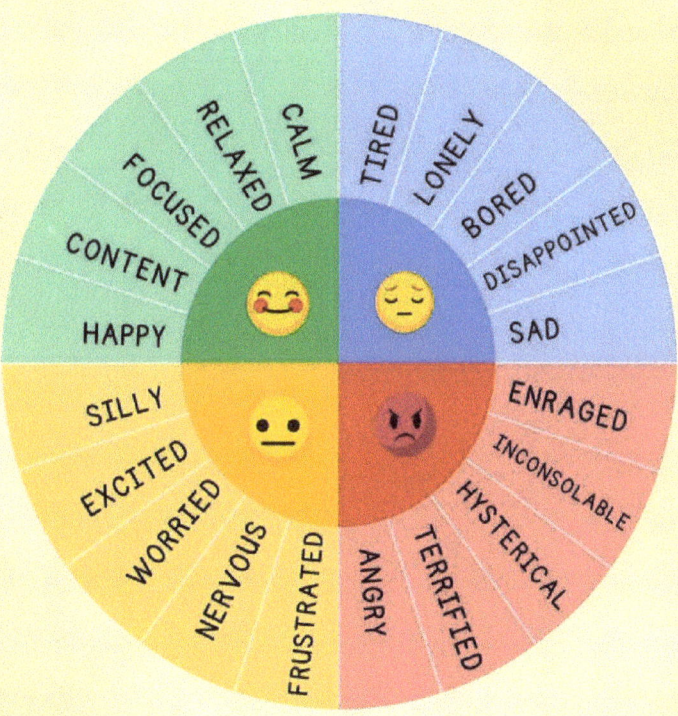

Positive Reminder:

Remember, focusing on gratitude can help shift your perspective. You have the power to see the good in your life.

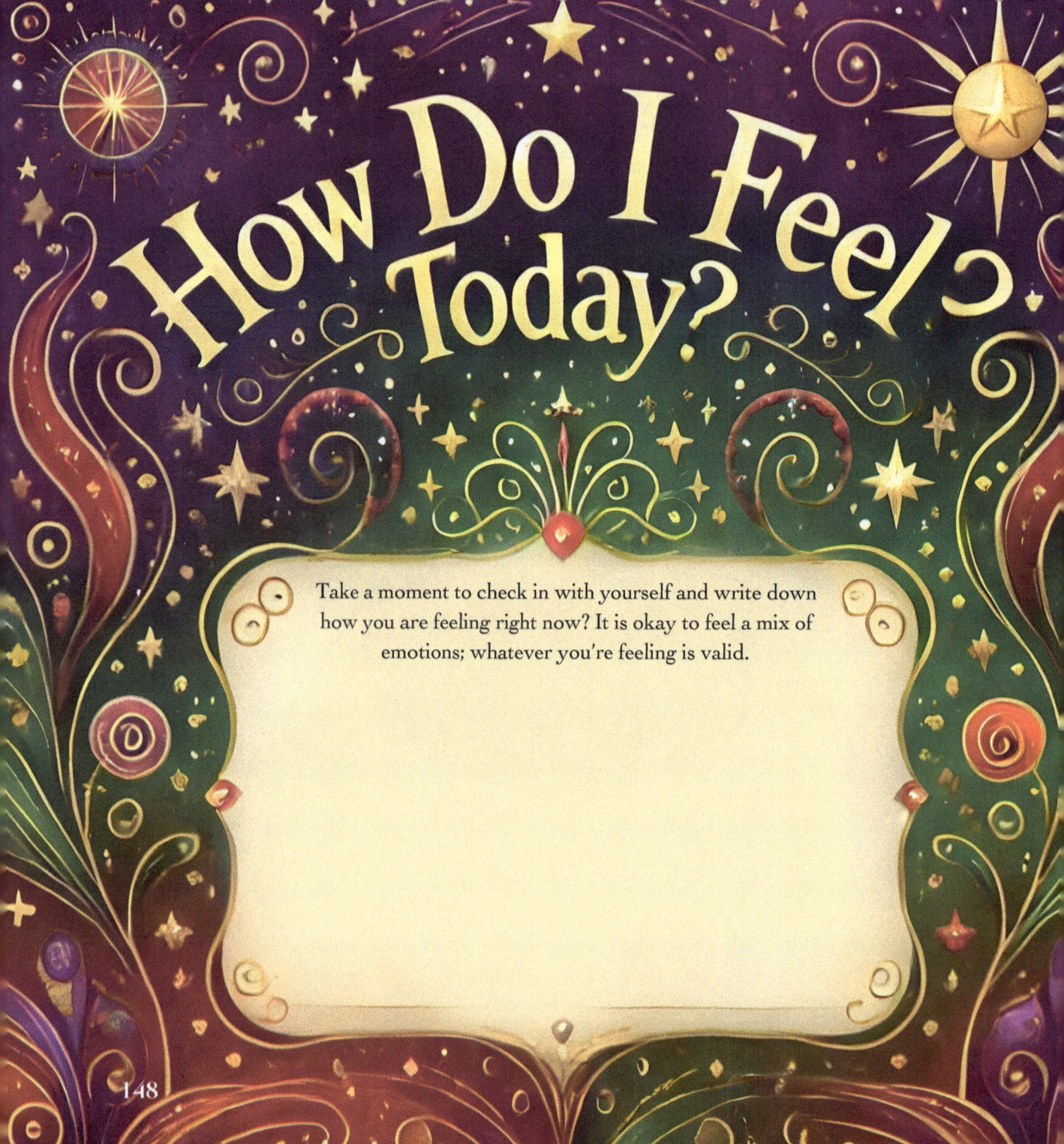

POSITIVE THOUGHTS

Whenever you need a little encouragement, turn to these inspiring and powerful messages that will help you see the beauty in every moment. You'll learn how to turn challenges into stepping stones and discover the magic of believing in yourself.

Positive Thoughts

1. Gratitude Changes How We See The World
When we focus on what we are grateful for, even the simplest things feel special; a sunny day, day, a nice talk, a wave from a friend, can make a big difference.

2. Happiness Comes From Appreciation, Not Perfection
You do not need everything to be perfect to be happy. Finding joy in small things is what truly brings peace.

3. Even Challenges Have Hidden Gifts
Sometimes, tough times teach us important lessons. Looking for the good in every situation helps us grow.

4. Gratitude Makes Life Brighter
The more we appreciate what we have, the more happiness we invite into our lives.

5. Every Day Brings Something To Be Thankful For
Even on difficult days, there is always something to appreciate: warm sunlight, a good meal, or a friend who listens.

Positive Thoughts

6. Saying Thank You Spreads Kindness
When we express gratitude, we not only feel better ourselves but also make others feel valued and appreciated.

7. Focusing On What We Have Brings More Joy
Instead of thinking about what is missing, notice what is already in your life. Gratitude turns "not enough" into "more than enough."

8. Little Things Hold Big Magic
The smell of rain, laughter, or a cozy blanket; life's small moments are often the most meaningful.

9. A Grateful Heart Brings Inner Peace
Appreciation helps us stop worrying about what we cannot control and enjoy what we do have.

10. Gratitude Is A Daily Practice
The more you practice being thankful, the easier it becomes to see the good in everything.

AFFIRMATIONS

1. I choose to focus on what I have, not what I lack.
2. There is always something to be grateful for.
3. I appreciate the small moments that bring me joy.
4. Gratitude fills my heart and brings me peace.
5. I see beauty in everyday life.
6. I am thankful for the love and kindness around me.
7. The more I appreciate, the more happiness I feel.
8. I recognise the good, even in difficult times.
9. Saying "thank you" spreads kindness.
10. Gratitude makes my heart feel full and my mind feel light.

Interactive Reflections

Journaling Prompt:
Think of a time when someone showed kindness to you. How did it make you feel?

Friend Connection:
Think of a friend who has done something kind for you. Write them a thank-you note to show your appreciation.

Interactive Reflections

Reflection Questions:
How does practising gratitude change your perspective?

What are some ways you can incorporate gratitude into your daily routine?

Weekly Challenge:
Each day this week, write down one thing you are grateful for in a journal. At the end of the week, reflect on how it made you feel.

Activity Page

Write down five things you're grateful for today.
They can be big or small.

YOUR OWN AFFIRMATION

Write Your Own Affirmations

WRITE Something Kind ABOUT YOURSELF

Ask My Heart

Your Heart Knows The Way

Deep inside you, there is a place where all the answers live, a place of kindness, and truth. That place is your heart.
It understands your worries, your dreams, and your deepest feelings.
When you're unsure, overwhelmed, or just need a friend, your heart is always there to listen.
Put your hand on your heart and take a deep breath. Your heart is always listening, always here for you. Whenever you need help, guidance, or just a moment of comfort, ask your heart.
Become friends with your heart, trust it, and share your thoughts and feelings.
Write down your questions, tell your heart about your day, and listen for what it has to say.
Your heart is your guide, always ready to help you find your way.

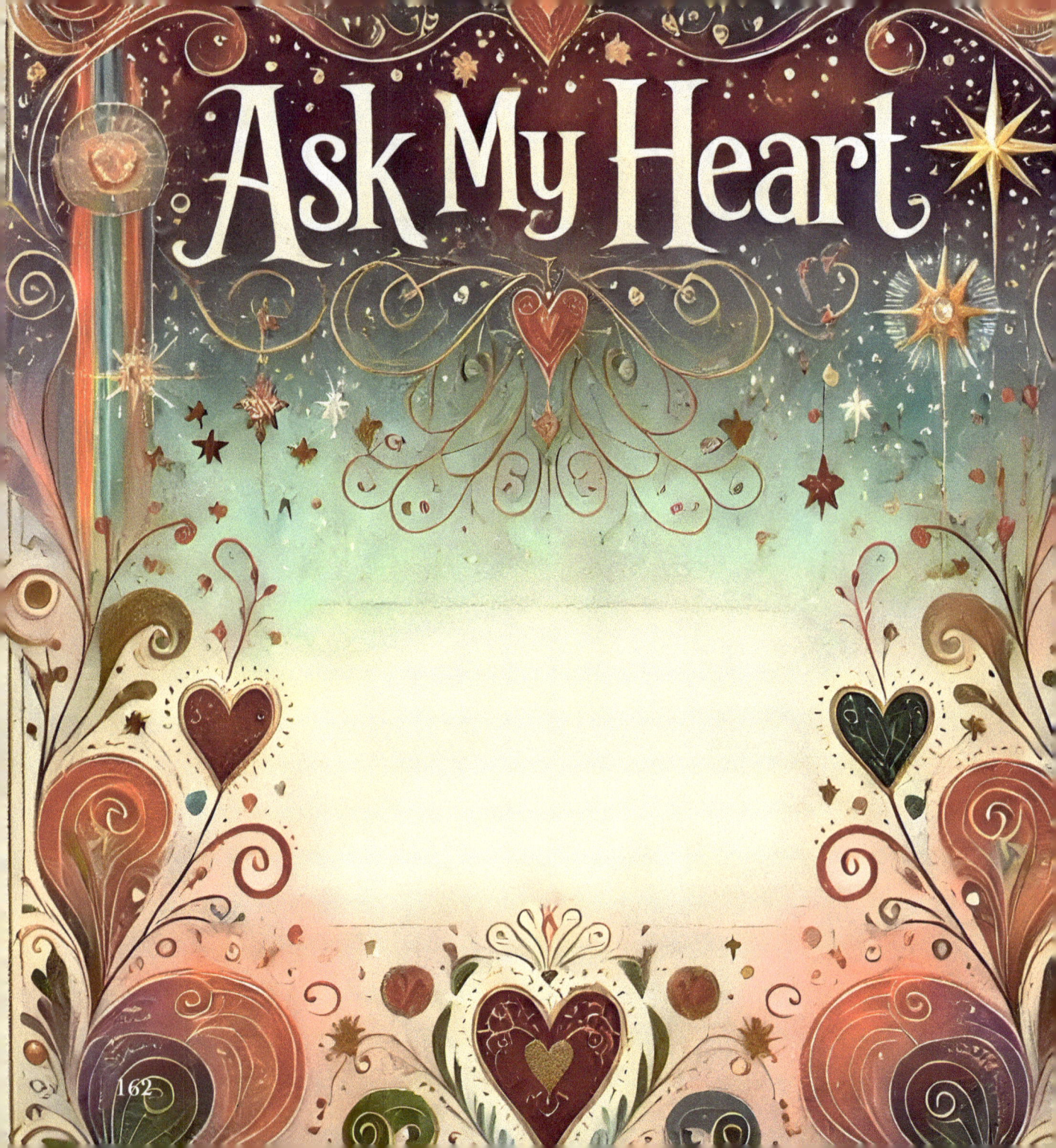

BEDTIME THOUGHTS

For Relaxation & Calm

Gentle Reflection & Gratitude
Think of someone who makes you feel truly loved. Imagine receiving a warm, comforting hug from them. Carry that love with you as you drift off.

Comforting Words
Even on the toughest days, you are never alone. You are surrounded by love, kindness, and caring hearts.

Positive Affirmations
"I am loved. I am important. I am safe."

BEDTIME THOUGHTS

For Relaxation & Calm

My Prayers
Take a moment to connect with Grace and Love. Whether you believe in God, Angels, or a Divine power, know that you are lovingly watched over. Offer your prayers and feel the peace that comes from being heard and supported.

Simple Breathing Exercise
Breathe in as if you're smelling a fresh flower, now exhale as if you're gently blowing out a candle. Continue this several times until you feel completely at ease.

A Short Visualisation
Picture yourself in a lovely cabin nestled in the woods. A soft blanket, the whispering wind, and a warm glow make you feel safe, calm, and ready for sleep.

My Dear Heart

You are always with me, always listening, always knowing what I need. You hold my dreams, my worries, my joys, and my questions. When I feel lost, you help me find my way. When I am unsure, you remind me of what truly matters.

I will learn to listen to you, to trust you, and to ask for your guidance. You are my friend, my safe place, my quiet strength.

Now, I will take a deep breath, put my hand on my heart, and ask, what do you want to tell me today?

Write your thoughts here or on a piece of paper.

My Dear Heart

My Notes

CHAPTER 7
CONFIDENCE BEGINS WITHIN

(For When You Are Feeling Unsure Of Yourself)

Opening Reflection

Confidence doesn't come from being perfect; it comes from believing in yourself, even when things are uncertain. No one else has your exact talents, thoughts, and wishes. This chapter will help you trust yourself, embrace your strengths, and know that you are capable of great things.

Emotion Wheel Activity

Now, take a moment to look at the section of the Emotion Wheel that represents how you feel right now. This can help you connect with your emotions and express them.

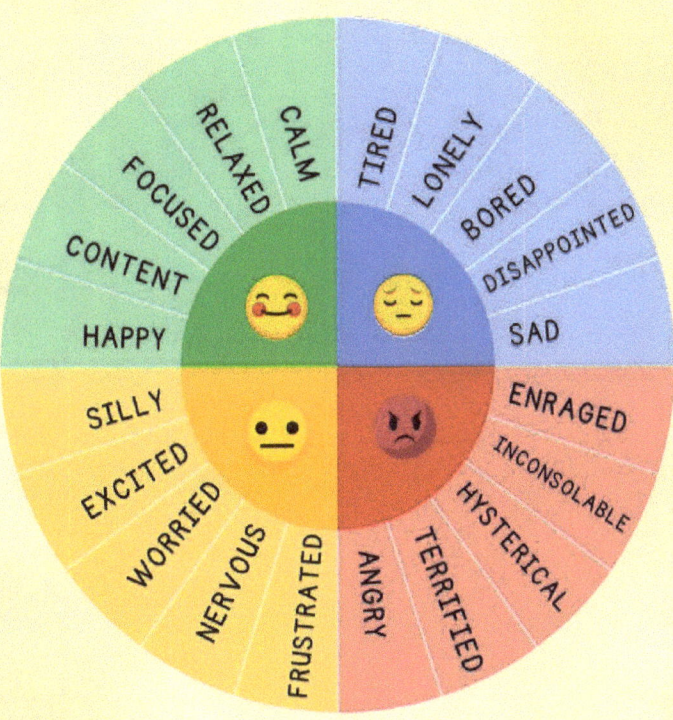

Positive Reminder:

Remember, confidence is built over time, and you have what it takes to believe in yourself.

How Do I Feel Today?

Take a moment to check in with yourself and write down how you are feeling right now? It is okay to feel a mix of emotions; whatever you're feeling is valid.

POSITIVE THOUGHTS

Whenever you need a little encouragement, turn to these inspiring and powerful messages that will help you see the beauty in every moment. You'll learn how to turn challenges into stepping stones and discover the magic of believing in yourself.

Positive Thoughts

1. Confidence Is Built, Not Born
No one is born feeling confident all the time. It grows every time you try, learn, and believe in yourself.

2. Mistakes Help You Learn
Confidence is not about never making mistakes; it is about knowing that mistakes help you grow.

3. You Are Your Own Biggest Supporter
What you say to yourself matters. Treat yourself like you would a best friend, with kindness and encouragement.

4. Your Strengths Are Unique
No one else sees the world exactly like you do. The things that make you different are also what make you special.

5. You Can Do Hard Things
Even when something feels scary, you have the ability to try, learn, and succeed.

Positive Thoughts

6. Confidence Comes From Taking Action
The more you try new things, the stronger your belief in yourself will become.

7. You Deserve To Take Up Space
You do not have to shrink yourself to fit in. Your voice and ideas matter.

8. Trust Yourself
You know more than you think. Believe in your ability to make good choices.

9. Challenges Help You Grow Stronger
Each time you step outside your comfort zone, your confidence grows.

10. The More You Believe in Yourself, The More Others Will Too
Confidence shines from the inside out. The way you see yourself influences how others see you.

AFFIRMATIONS

1. I believe in myself and my abilities.
2. I am proud of who I am.
3. I am capable of achieving great things.
4. My voice matters.
5. I grow stronger every time I try something new.
6. I do not have to be perfect to be valuable.
7. I trust myself to make good decisions.
8. I deserve to be seen and heard.
9. I am learning, growing, and becoming my best self.
10. Confidence starts with me, and I choose to believe in myself.

Interactive Reflections

Journaling Prompt:
What is one thing you'd try if you believed in yourself fully?

Friend Connection:
Share your "I Am" statements with a friend. Encourage them to do the same and celebrate each other's strengths.

Interactive Reflections

Reflection Questions:
When have you felt most confident in yourself?

How can you remind yourself of your strengths during challenging times?

Weekly Challenge:
This week, try one new activity or skill that you have wanted to explore, even if it makes you feel a little nervous. Reflect on how it felt afterward.

ACTIVITY PAGE

Write down three things you are good at or proud of. They can be skills, personality traits, or things you've accomplished.

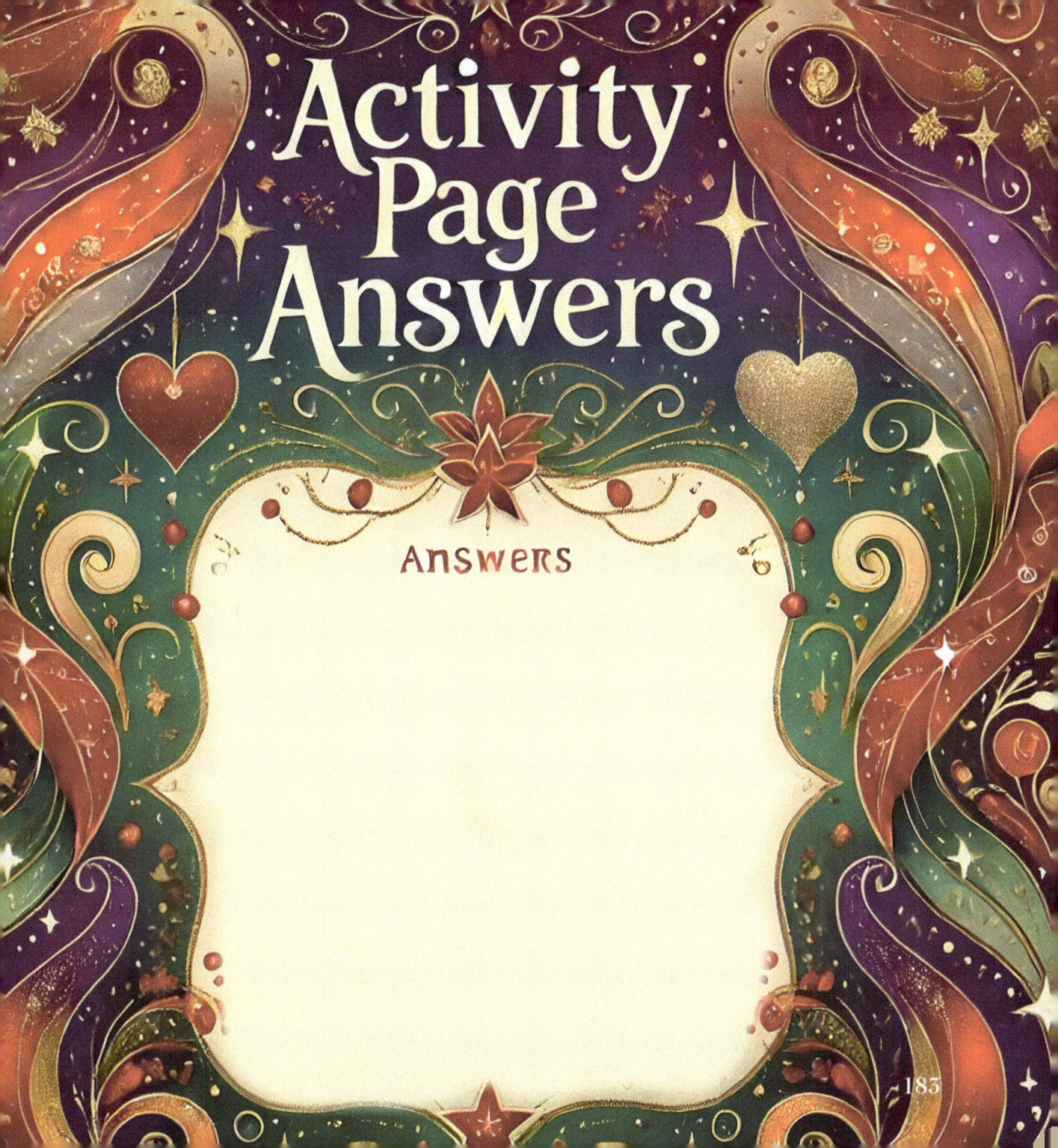

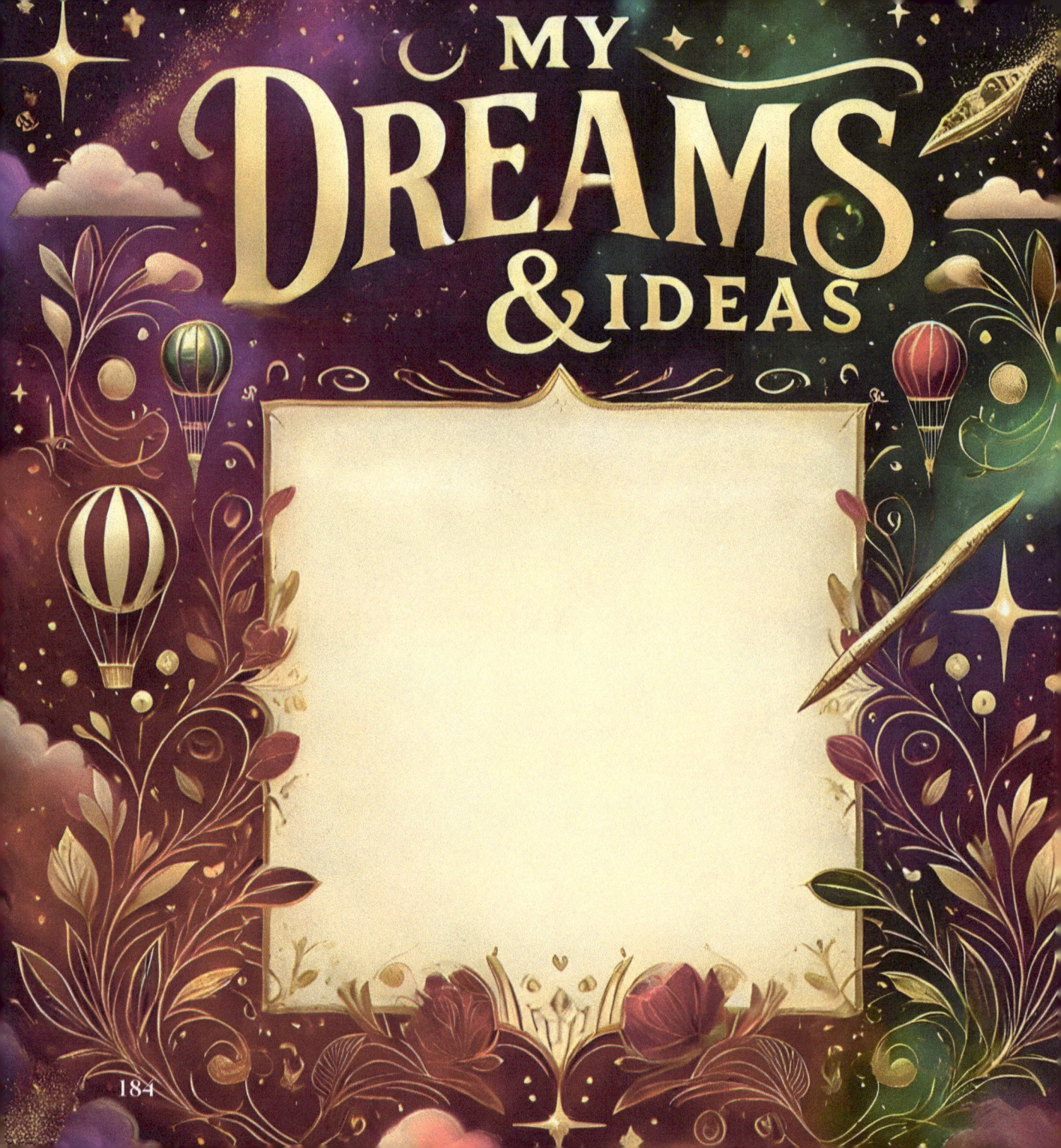

Write Something Kind About Yourself

Ask My Heart

Your Heart Knows The Way

Deep inside you, there is a place where all the answers live, a place of kindness, and truth. That place is your heart.
It understands your worries, your dreams, and your deepest feelings. When you're unsure, overwhelmed, or just need a friend, your heart is always there to listen.
Put your hand on your heart and take a deep breath. Your heart is always listening, always here for you. Whenever you need help, guidance, or just a moment of comfort, ask your heart.
Become friends with your heart, trust it, and share your thoughts and feelings.
Write down your questions, tell your heart about your day, and listen for what it has to say.
Your heart is your guide, always ready to help you find your way.

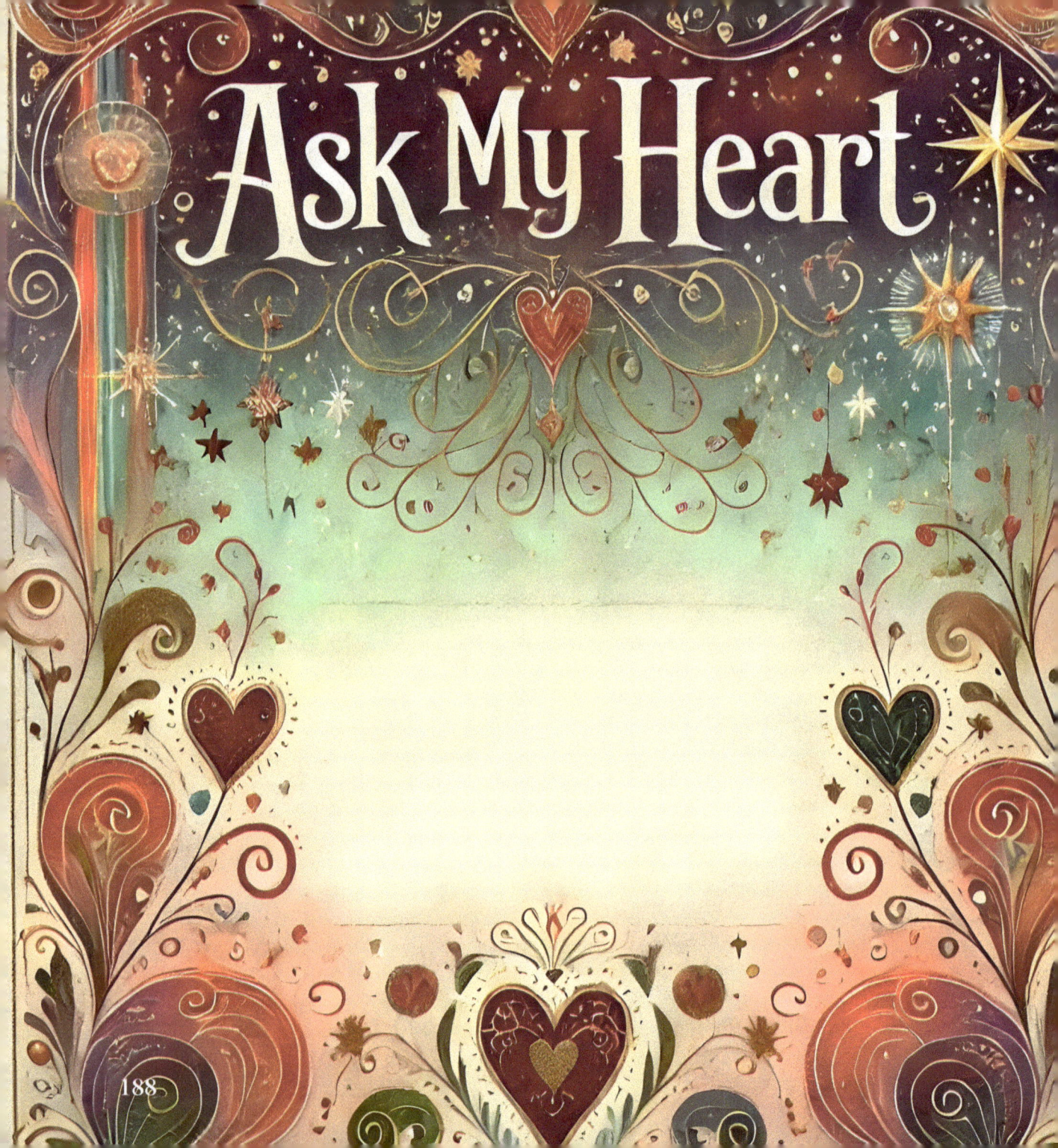

BEDTIME THOUGHTS

For Relaxation & Calm

Gentle Reflection & Gratitude
Recall a peaceful moment from today, a quiet sky, a shared laugh, or the warmth of the sun. Let that peace settle in your heart.

Comforting Words
Everything is okay. Right now, you don't have to be anywhere or do anything. Just relax and allow yourself to rest.

Positive Affirmations
"I am unique. I am strong. I am exactly where I need to be."

BEDTIME THOUGHTS

For Relaxation & Calm

My Prayers
Take a moment to connect with Grace and Love. Whether you believe in God, Angels, or a Divine power, know that you are lovingly watched over. Offer your prayers and feel the peace that comes from being heard and supported.

Simple Breathing Exercise
Breathe in slowly through your nose, hold for a moment, then exhale gently through your mouth, feeling your body relax.

A Short Visualisation
Imagine lying on a serene beach. The gentle waves wash ashore, and the sound of the ocean calms your mind as you fall sleep.

My Dear Heart

You are always with me, always listening, always knowing what I need. You hold my dreams, my worries, my joys, and my questions. When I feel lost, you help me find my way. When I am unsure, you remind me of what truly matters.

I will learn to listen to you, to trust you, and to ask for your guidance. You are my friend, my safe place, my quiet strength.

Now, I will take a deep breath, put my hand on my heart, and ask, what do you want to tell me today?

Write your thoughts here or on a piece of paper.

My Dear Heart

My Notes

CHAPTER 8
BOUNCING BACK

(or When You Are Dealing With Mistakes Or Disappointments)

Opening Reflection

Sometimes things don't go as planned. Maybe you didn't succeed at something you worked hard for, or you feel like you let yourself or others down. It is okay. Failure is not the opposite of success; it's part of the journey. Every setback teaches you something valuable and helps you grow stronger. This chapter will remind you that mistakes don't define you.

Emotion Wheel Activity

Now, take a moment to look at the section of the Emotion Wheel that represents how you feel right now. This can help you connect with your emotions and express them.

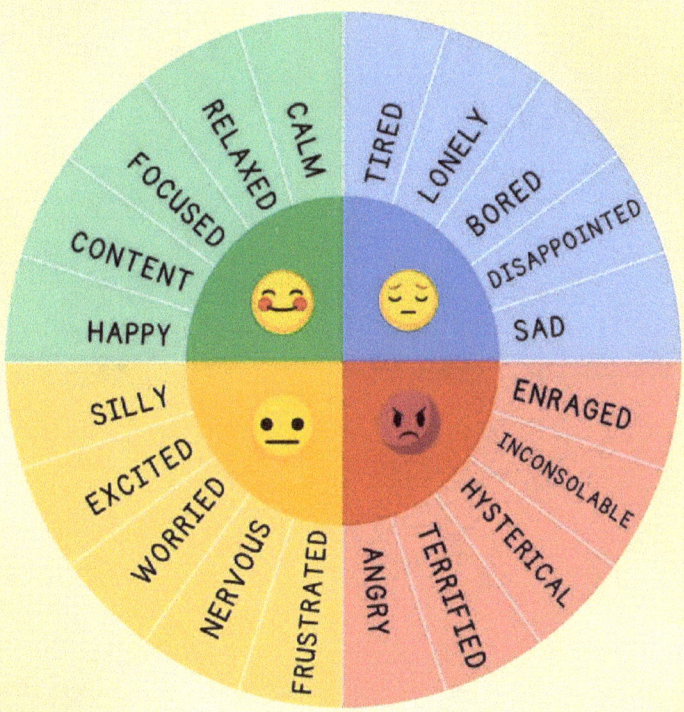

Positive Reminder:

Remember, failure is a part of learning. You have the resilience to rise again.

How Do I Feel Today?

Take a moment to check in with yourself and write down how you are feeling right now? It is okay to feel a mix of emotions; whatever you're feeling is valid.

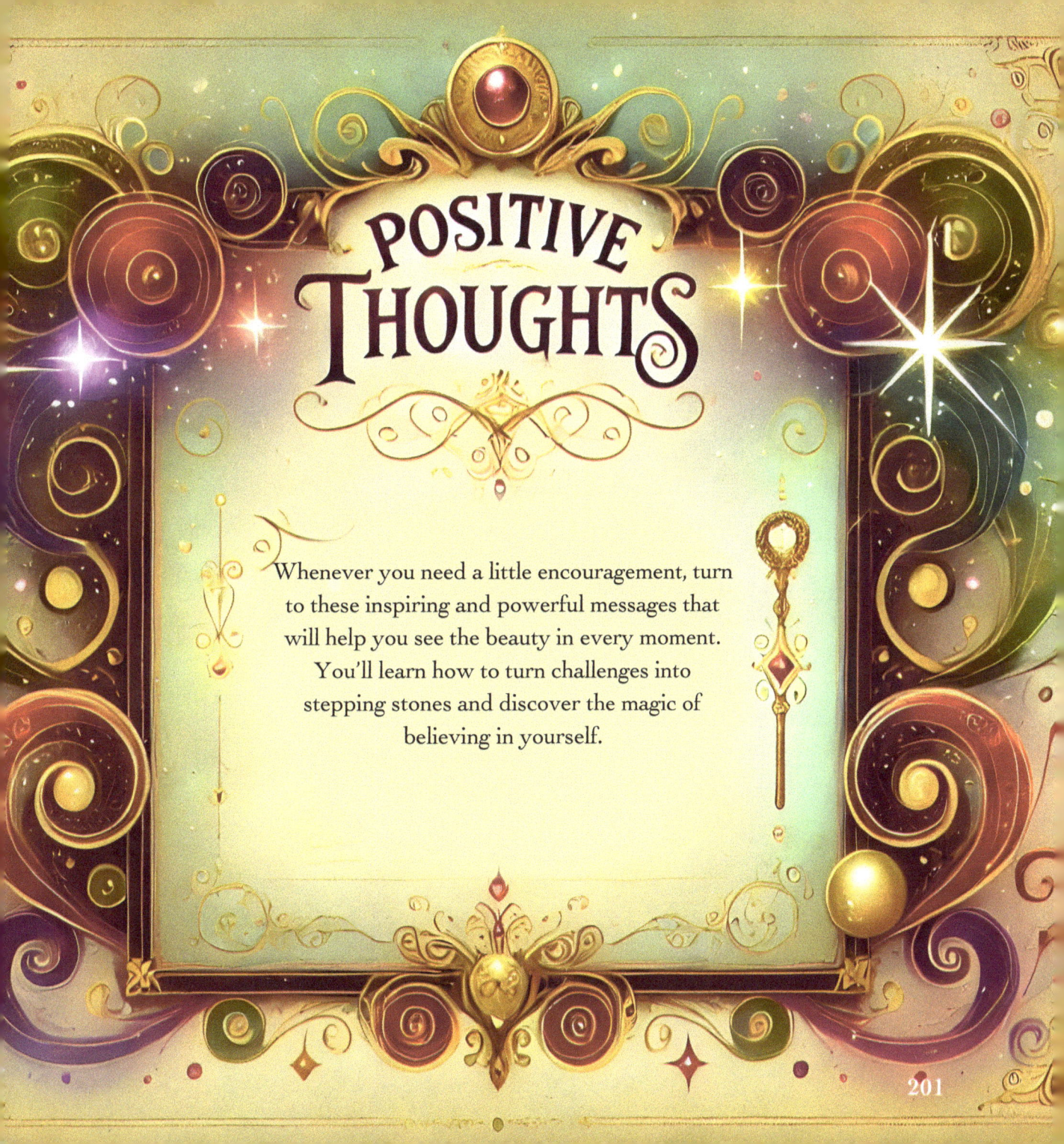

POSITIVE THOUGHTS

Whenever you need a little encouragement, turn to these inspiring and powerful messages that will help you see the beauty in every moment. You'll learn how to turn challenges into stepping stones and discover the magic of believing in yourself.

Positive Thoughts

1. Failure Is Proof That You Tried
Making mistakes means you were brave enough to try. That alone is something to be proud of.

2. Every Setback Holds A Lesson
Think of failure as a teacher. What can this moment teach you? What would you do differently next time?

3. You Are Not Your Mistakes
A mistake is something that happens; it is not who you are. You are always growing and learning.

4. Even The Best Have Made Mistakes
Every successful person has faced making a mistake. What makes them great is that they didn't give up.

5. You Are Stronger Than This Moment
Right now, it may feel hard, but this feeling will pass. You have overcome tough times before, and you will again.

Positive Thoughts

6. Disappointment Means You Care
Feeling upset means you had hope and dreams. That is a good thing; it means you're passionate about something.

7. Success Comes From Keep Trying
You don't have to get everything right the first time. The key is to keep going.

8. You Can Always Start Again
Every day is a new chance to try, improve, and move forward.

9. Your Effort Matters
Even if things did not turn out as expected, the effort you put in still counts.

10. You Will Look Back and See Growth
One day, this moment will be a lesson that helped shape you into who you are becoming.

AFFIRMATIONS

1. I am not my mistakes; I am always learning and growing.
2. Every challenge makes me stronger.
3. I give myself permission to try again.
4. Setbacks do not define me; my effort does.
5. I choose to focus on what I can learn.
6. I am proud of myself for trying.
7. I am resilient and capable of overcoming challenges.
8. Every day is a new chance to improve.
9. I let go of disappointment and move forward.
10. I believe in myself, no matter what.

Interactive Reflections

Journaling Prompt:
If you knew that making a mistake was not something to fear, what would you try?

Friend Connection:
If a friend is feeling down about a failure, how can you remind them that it is part of the journey? Write down a supportive phrase you can share.

Interactive Reflections

Reflection Questions:
What did you learn from a recent disappointment?

How can you remind yourself that making mistakes is a natural part of growth?

Weekly Challenge:
This week, find one area in your life where you want to improve. Set a small goal and work towards it, noting any mistakes as part of the learning process.

ACTIVITY PAGE

Write down one time you made a mistake but later realised it helped you learn or grow.

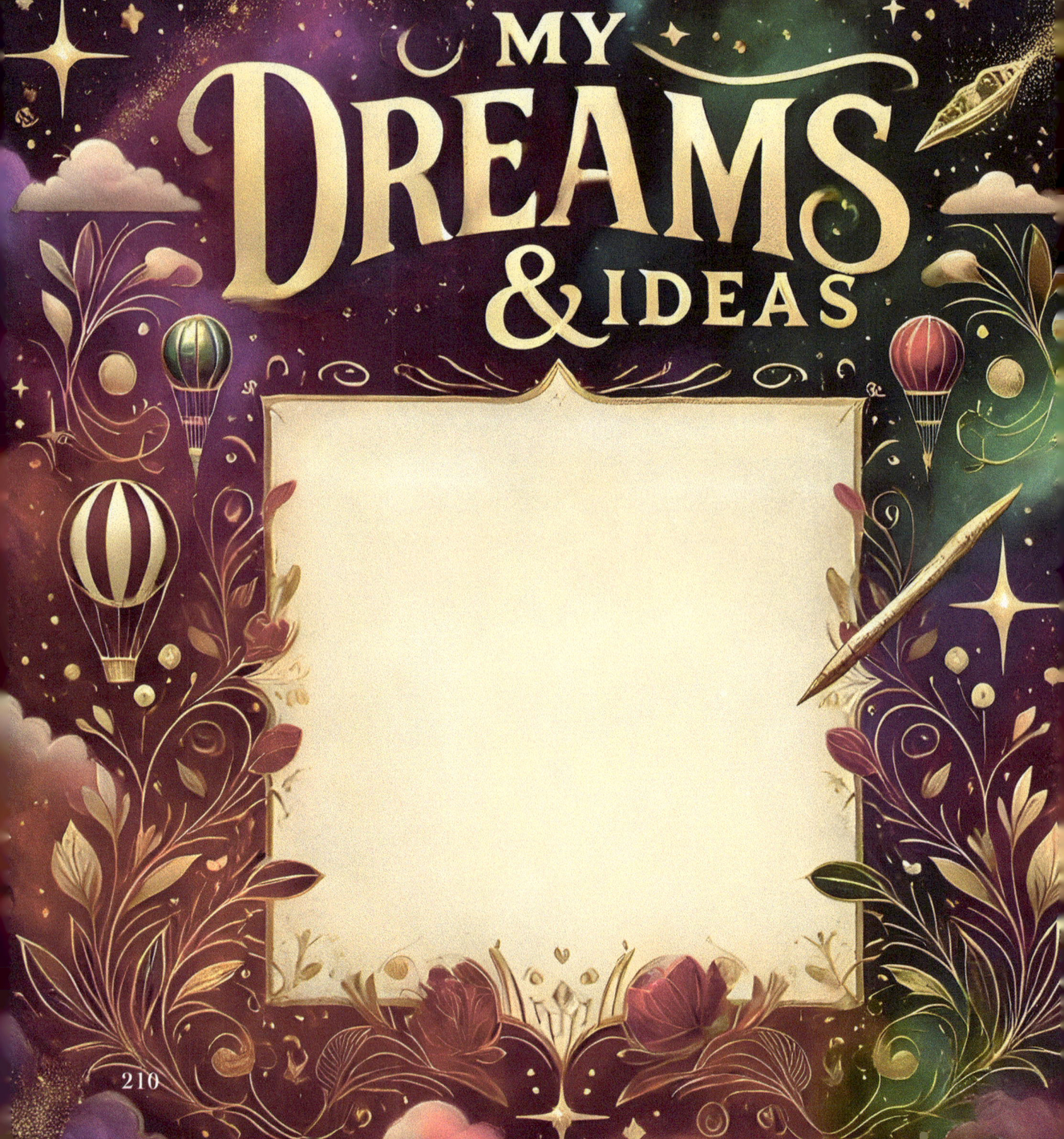

YOUR OWN AFFIRMATION

Write Your Own Affirmations

Ask My Heart

Your Heart Knows The Way

Deep inside you, there is a place where all the answers live, a place of kindness, and truth. That place is your heart.
It understands your worries, your dreams, and your deepest feelings. When you're unsure, overwhelmed, or just need a friend, your heart is always there to listen.
Put your hand on your heart and take a deep breath. Your heart is always listening, always here for you. Whenever you need help, guidance, or just a moment of comfort, ask your heart.
Become friends with your heart, trust it, and share your thoughts and feelings.
Write down your questions, tell your heart about your day, and listen for what it has to say.
Your heart is your guide, always ready to help you find your way.

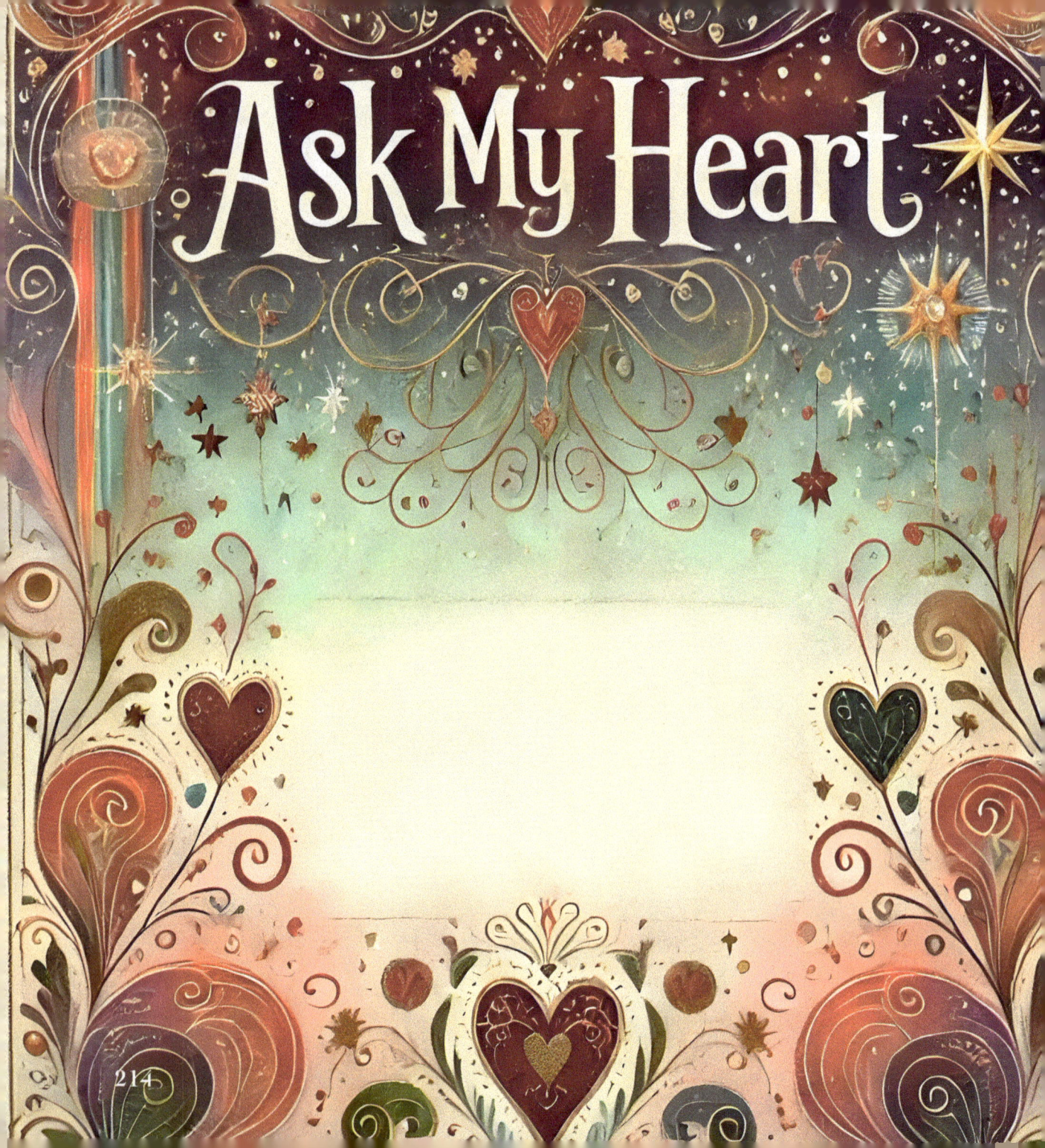

BEDTIME THOUGHTS

For Relaxation & Calm

Gentle Reflection & Gratitude
Think of one thing you're looking forward to, no matter how small. It might be a favourite breakfast, a fun activity, or spending time with someone special. Let that excitement fill your heart as you drift off.

Comforting Words
No matter what happened today, tomorrow is a fresh start. Countless possibilities await you.

Positive Affirmations
"I am hopeful. I am capable. I am ready for a new day."

BEDTIME THOUGHTS

For Relaxation & Calm

My Prayers
Take a moment to connect with Grace and Love. Whether you believe in God, Angels, or a Divine power, know that you are lovingly watched over. Offer your prayers and feel the peace that comes from being heard and supported.

Simple Breathing Exercise
Breathe in deeply, imagining yourself filling with bright, positive light. Now exhale slowly, releasing any heaviness from the day. Do this several times until you feel calm.

A Short Visualisation
Visualise a field dotted with soft, glowing fireflies. Their gentle light wraps you in warmth, guiding you into a night of peaceful dreams.

My Dear Heart

You are always with me, always listening, always knowing what I need. You hold my dreams, my worries, my joys, and my questions. When I feel lost, you help me find my way. When I am unsure, you remind me of what truly matters.

I will learn to listen to you, to trust you, and to ask for your guidance. You are my friend, my safe place, my quiet strength.

Now, I will take a deep breath, put my hand on my heart, and ask, what do you want to tell me today?

Write your thoughts here or on a piece of paper.

My Dear Heart

My Notes

CHAPTER 9

You Are Loved Just As You Are

(For When You Are Feeling Lonely Or Left Out)

Opening
REFLECTION

Loneliness can feel heavy, like you do not belong or like no one understands you. But you are never truly alone. Even in moments of loneliness, love is all around you; you just might not see it yet. This is a reminder that you are valued, important, and deeply loved, exactly as you are.

Emotion Wheel Activity

Now, take a moment to look at the section of the Emotion Wheel that represents how you feel right now. This can help you connect with your emotions and express them.

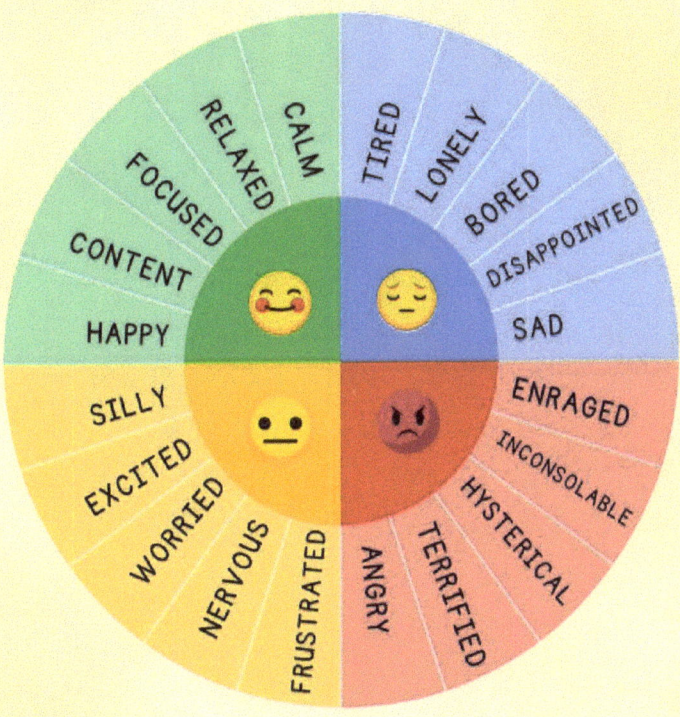

Positive Reminder:

Remember, you are loved just as you are. You belong, and your feelings matter.

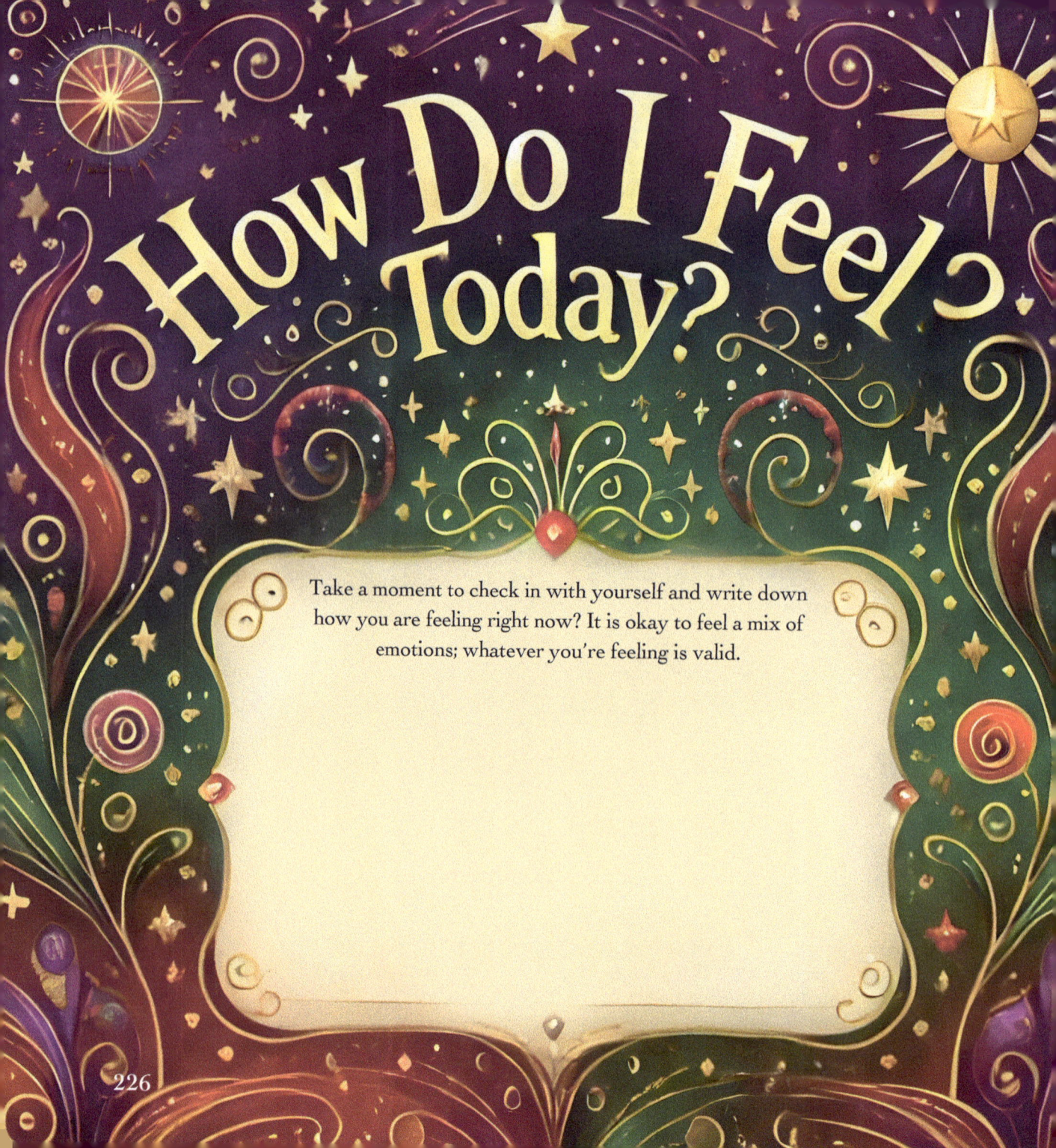

How Do I Feel Today?

Take a moment to check in with yourself and write down how you are feeling right now? It is okay to feel a mix of emotions; whatever you're feeling is valid.

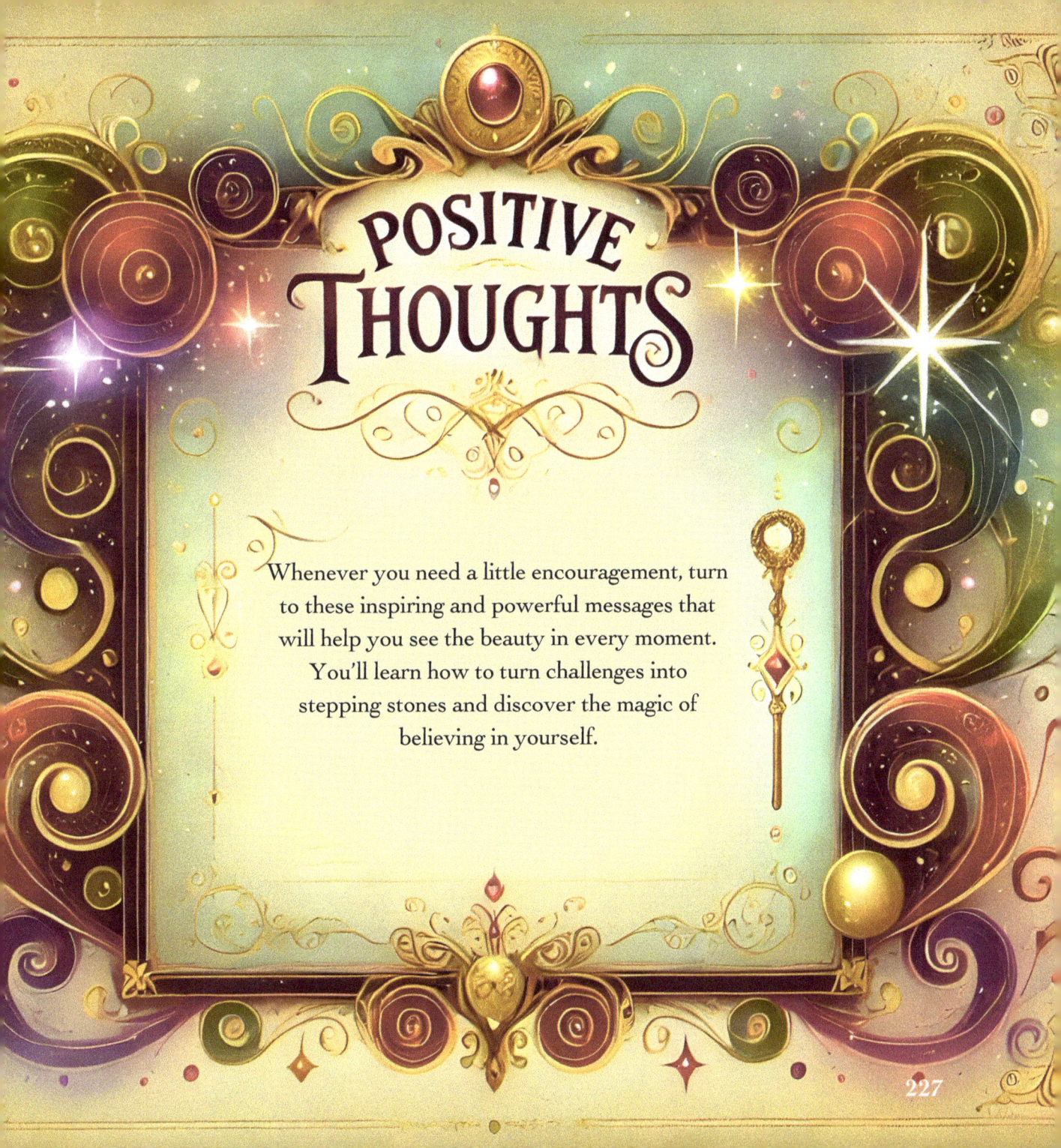

POSITIVE THOUGHTS

Whenever you need a little encouragement, turn to these inspiring and powerful messages that will help you see the beauty in every moment. You'll learn how to turn challenges into stepping stones and discover the magic of believing in yourself.

Positive Thoughts

1. You Are Enough, Just As You Are
You do not have to change to be loved. The right people will appreciate you for who you are.

2. Feeling Lonely Does Not Mean You Are Alone
Even if you feel lonely, there are people who care about you and want to support you.

3. You Belong In This World
There is no one else like you, and that makes you special. You have a place in this world.

4. Friendships Take Time
If you feel left out, remember that friendships grow over time. Keep being yourself, and the right people will find you.

5. Love Comes In Many Forms
Love is not just about friends; it can come from family, pets, teachers, and even yourself.

Positive Thoughts

6. You Can Be Your Own Best Friend
The most important relationship you will ever have is with yourself. Speak to yourself with kindness.

7. Even One Person Can Make A Difference
If you feel alone, reach out to someone, a friend, family member, or teacher. Connection starts with one step.

8. You Are Always Loved, Even When You Cannot See It
Just because you do not feel love in this moment doesn't mean it's not there. Love surrounds you in ways you may not realise.

9. You Are Worthy Of Love and Friendship
You do not have to earn love; you deserve it just by being you.

10. You Can Create Connection
Sometimes, making the first move, smiling, saying hello, or showing kindness, can open the door to new friendships.

Affirmations

1. I am loved and valued just as I am.
2. I belong in this world.
3. I am worthy of connection and friendship.
4. Love surrounds me, even when I do not see it.
5. I am enough, exactly as I am.
6. I have so much to offer the world.
7. I choose to be kind to myself.
8. I trust that the right people will find their way into my life.
9. I am never truly alone.
10. I deserve love, and I welcome it into my life.

Interactive Reflections

Journaling Prompt:
Think of someone who makes you feel valued. What do you appreciate about them?

Friend Connection:
If you notice a friend feeling left out, how can you invite them to join you? Write down one way to include them in your activities.

Interactive Reflections

Reflection Questions:
How can you remind yourself of your worth when you feel lonely?

What are some ways you can show love and kindness to yourself?

Weekly Challenge:
This week, reach out to someone you care about and tell them why you appreciate them. Then, take a moment to reflect on how it felt to connect.

Activity Page

Write a letter to yourself as if you were your best friend. What would you say to remind yourself that you are special?

YOUR OWN AFFIRMATION

Write Your Own Affirmations

WRITE Something Kind ABOUT YOURSELF

Ask My Heart

Your Heart Knows The Way

Deep inside you, there is a place where all the answers live, a place of kindness, and truth. That place is your heart.
It understands your worries, your dreams, and your deepest feelings.
When you're unsure, overwhelmed, or just need a friend, your heart is always there to listen.
Put your hand on your heart and take a deep breath. Your heart is always listening, always here for you. Whenever you need help, guidance, or just a moment of comfort, ask your heart.
Become friends with your heart, trust it, and share your thoughts and feelings.
Write down your questions, tell your heart about your day, and listen for what it has to say.
Your heart is your guide, always ready to help you find your way.

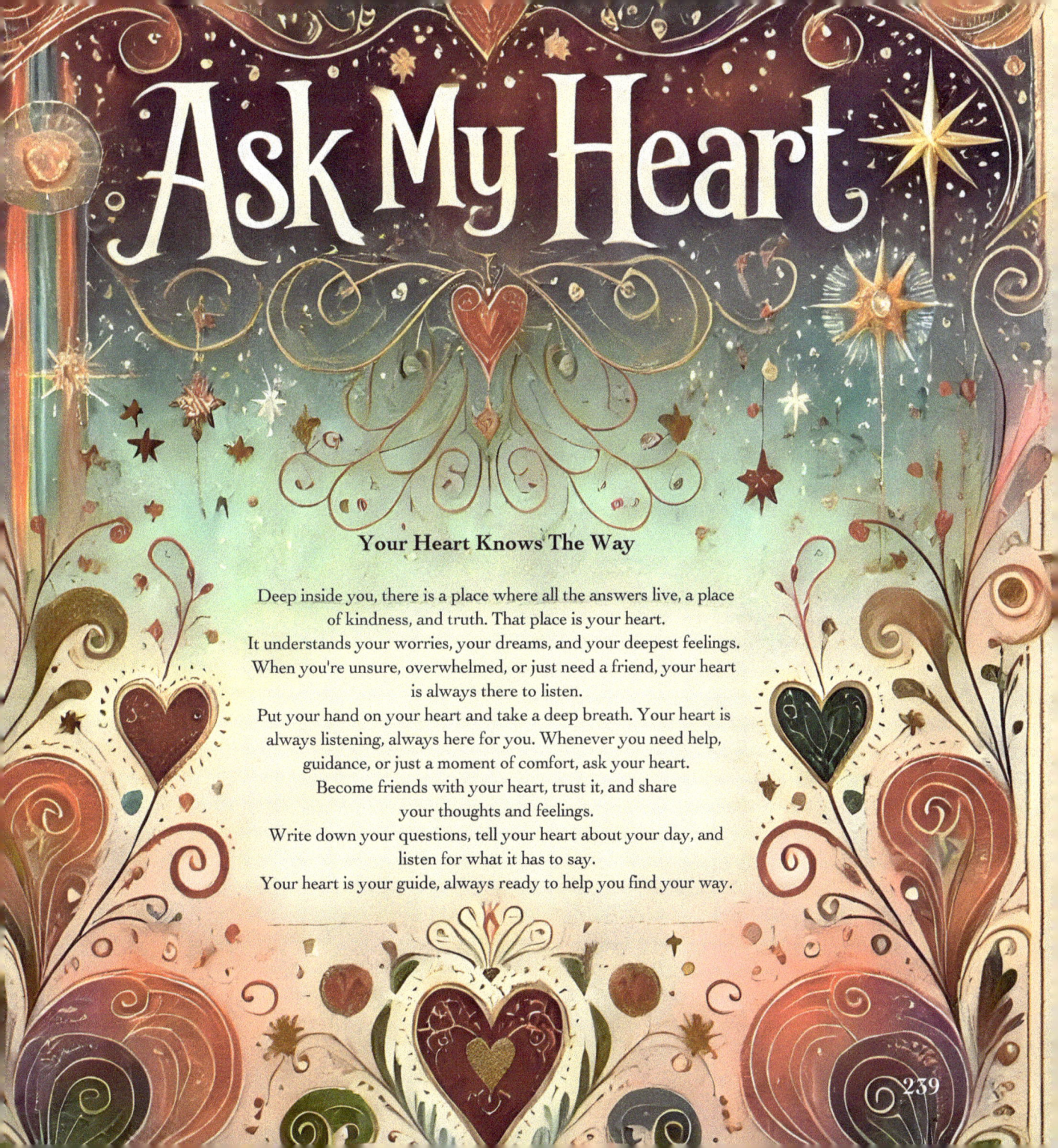

BEDTIME THOUGHTS

For Relaxation & Calm

Gentle Reflection & Gratitude
Think of a moment today when you felt proud of yourself. Perhaps you were kind, tried something new, or simply did your best. Hold that feeling close as you rest.

Comforting Words
You are enough. You are loved just as you are, and every step you take is meaningful.

Positive Affirmations
"I am proud of myself. I am growing. I am enough."

BEDTIME THOUGHTS

For Relaxation & Calm

My Prayers
Take a moment to connect with Grace and Love. Whether you believe in God, Angels, or a Divine power, know that you are lovingly watched over. Offer your prayers and feel the peace that comes from being heard and supported.

Simple Breathing Exercise
Breathe in deeply, imagining a warm, golden light filling you up. Exhale slowly, releasing stress and tension. Do this three times.

A Short Visualisation
Picture yourself gently floating on a soft, fluffy cloud, drifting high above, feeling light, safe, and embraced by calm.

My Dear Heart

You are always with me, always listening, always knowing what I need. You hold my dreams, my worries, my joys, and my questions. When I feel lost, you help me find my way. When I am unsure, you remind me of what truly matters.

I will learn to listen to you, to trust you, and to ask for your guidance. You are my friend, my safe place, my quiet strength.

Now, I will take a deep breath, put my hand on my heart, and ask, what do you want to tell me today?

Write your thoughts here or on a piece of paper.

My Dear Heart

My Notes

Chapter 10
Dream Big, Shine Bright

(For When You Need Motivation & Inspiration)

Opening Reflection

You have so many dreams inside you, things you want to do, places you want to go, goals you want to achieve. Sometimes, doubt or fear can get in the way, but don't let it stop you. This is a reminder that you are capable of amazing things and that your dreams are worth chasing.

Emotion Wheel Activity

Now, take a moment to look at the section of the Emotion Wheel that represents how you feel right now. This can help you connect with your emotions and express them.

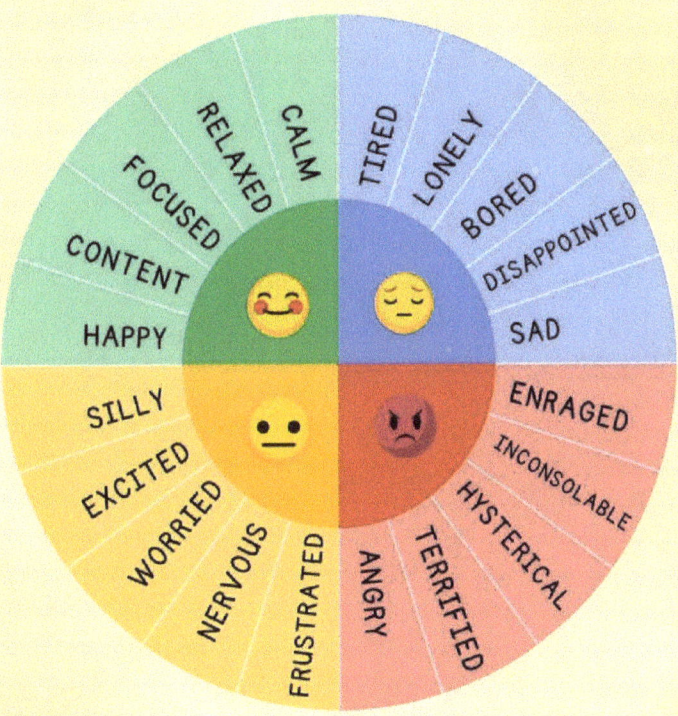

Positive Reminder:

Remember, your dreams matter, and you have the courage to pursue them.

How Do I Feel Today?

Take a moment to check in with yourself and write down how you are feeling right now? It is okay to feel a mix of emotions; whatever you're feeling is valid.

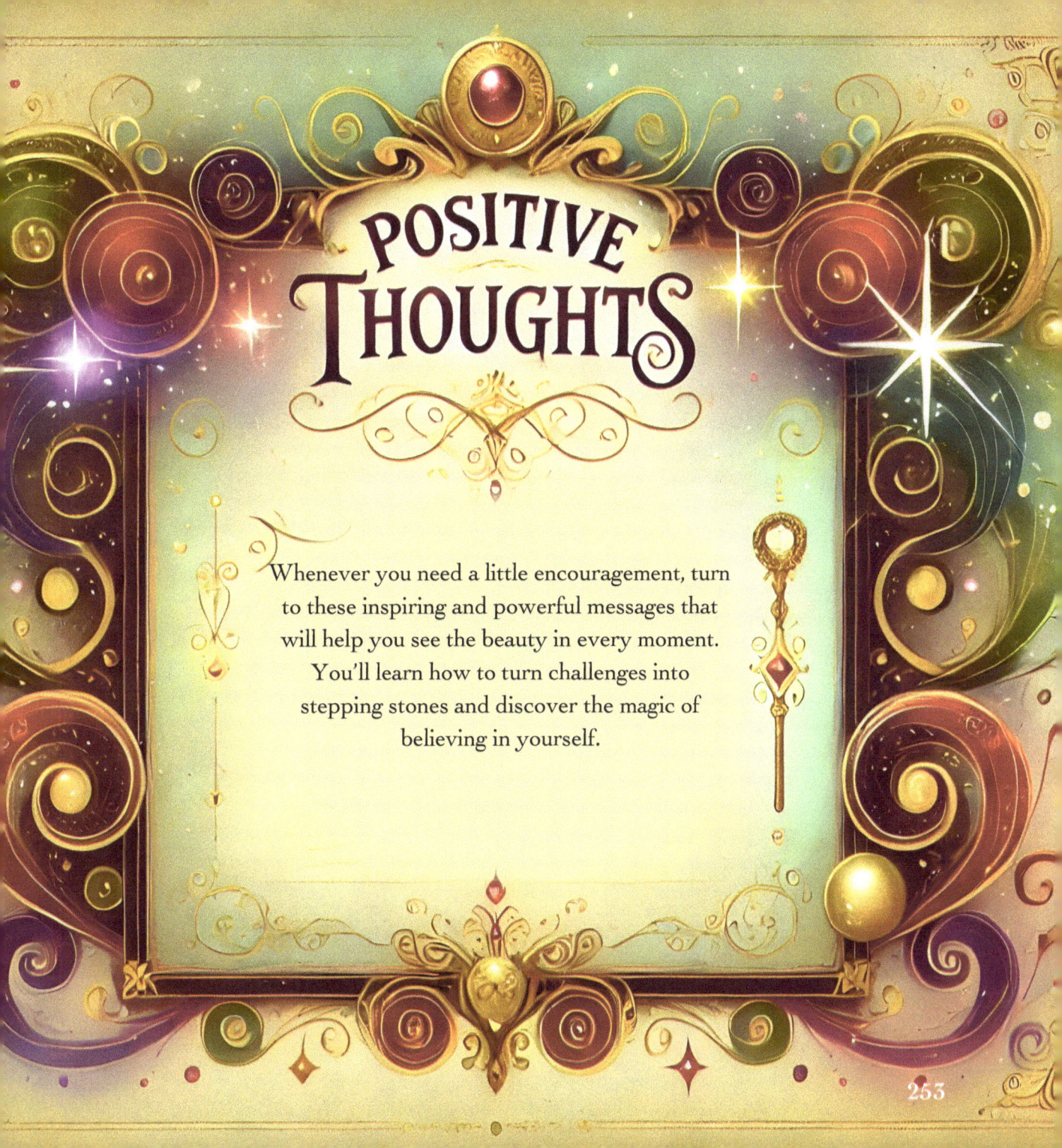

POSITIVE THOUGHTS

Whenever you need a little encouragement, turn to these inspiring and powerful messages that will help you see the beauty in every moment. You'll learn how to turn challenges into stepping stones and discover the magic of believing in yourself.

Positive Thoughts

1. Your Dreams Matter
What you want to do and become is important. Your dreams deserve to be followed.

2. Every Big Goal Starts Small
Every successful person started with a first step. Take one step toward your dream today.

3. You Are Capable Of Great Things
You have talents, strengths, and ideas that make you special. Believe in them.

4. Mistakes Are Part Of The Journey
No one succeeds without mistakes. Keep going, even when things do not go as planned.

5. Your Hard Work Will Pay Off
Every bit of effort you put in brings you closer to your goal.

Positive Thoughts

6. Your Dreams Inspire Others
When you go after what you love, you encourage others to do the same.

7. You Are Stronger Than Your Doubts
Doubt is just a thought; it doesn't control your future.

8. Success Looks Different For Everyone
Your path is your own. Keep going at your own pace.

9. Your Future Is Full Of Possibilities
There are endless paths ahead. You are capable of shaping your own future.

10. You Were Born To Shine
You have something unique to offer the world. Never stop believing in yourself.

AFFIRMATIONS

1. I believe in my dreams.
2. I am capable of achieving my goals.
3. I take small steps toward big success.
4. My efforts bring me closer to my dreams.
5. I trust my journey, even when it takes time.
6. Doubt does not define me; I believe in myself.
7. I have the power to create my future.
8. I am strong, determined, and capable.
9. My dreams are worth the effort.
10. I am ready to shine my light in the world.

Interactive Reflections

Journaling Prompt:
What is one small step you can take today toward your biggest dream?

Friend Connection:
Share your dreams with a friend and ask them about theirs. Write down one thing you can do together to support each other in achieving those dreams.

Interactive Reflections

Reflection Questions:
What is your biggest dream, and what steps can you take to achieve it?

How can you stay motivated when challenges arise?

Weekly Challenge:
This week, take time each day to visualise your dreams and write down one action step you can take toward achieving them.

Activity Page

Create a vision board with pictures, words, or drawings that represent your dreams.

YOUR OWN AFFIRMATION

Write Your Own Affirmations

Ask My Heart

Your Heart Knows The Way

Deep inside you, there is a place where all the answers live, a place
of kindness, and truth. That place is your heart.
It understands your worries, your dreams, and your deepest feelings.
When you're unsure, overwhelmed, or just need a friend, your heart
is always there to listen.
Put your hand on your heart and take a deep breath. Your heart is
always listening, always here for you. Whenever you need help,
guidance, or just a moment of comfort, ask your heart.
Become friends with your heart, trust it, and share
your thoughts and feelings.
Write down your questions, tell your heart about your day, and
listen for what it has to say.
Your heart is your guide, always ready to help you find your way.

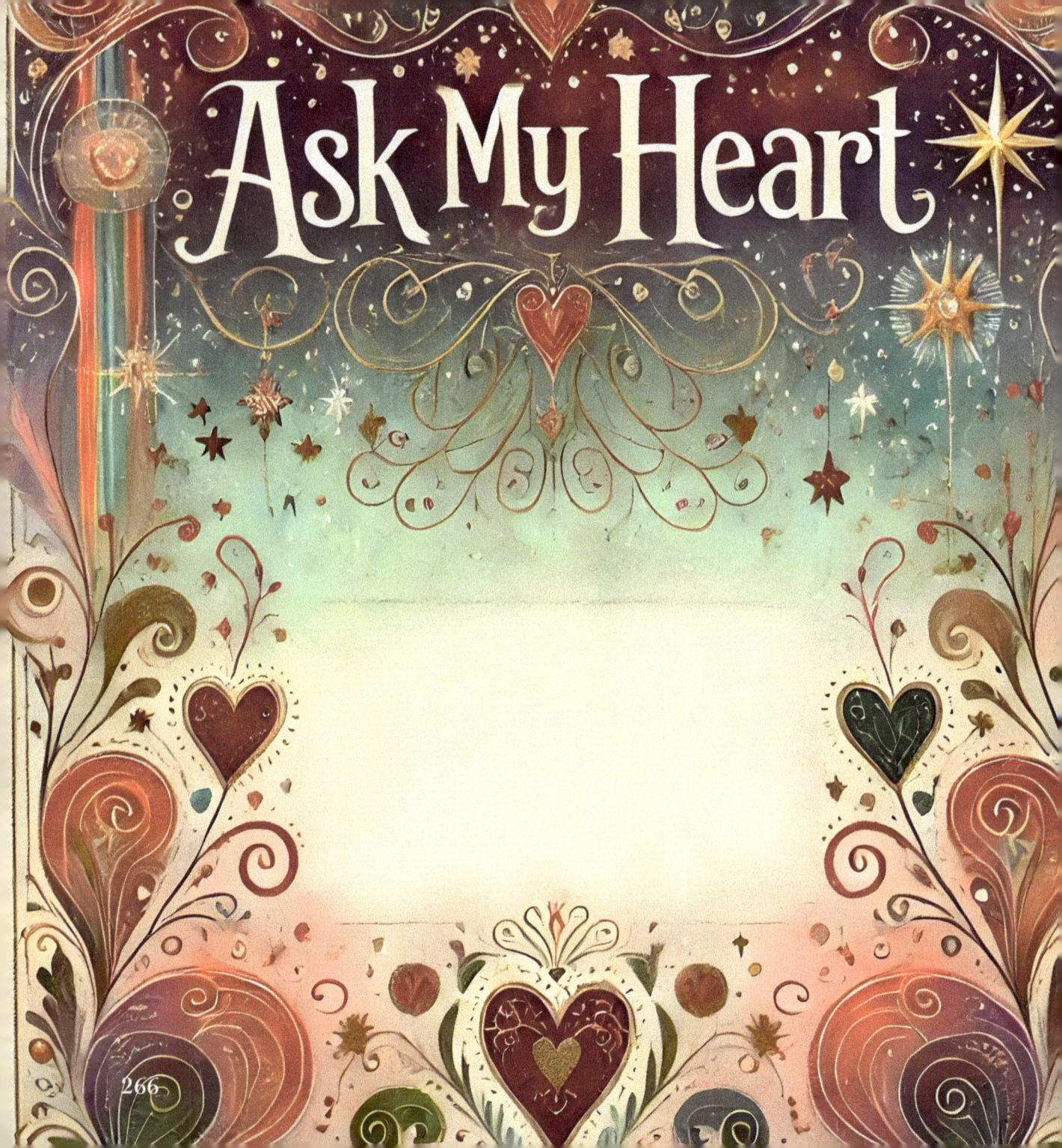

BEDTIME THOUGHTS

For Relaxation & Calm

Gentle Reflection & Gratitude
Reflect on one thing that brought you calm today, a quiet moment, a favourite song, or a deep, soothing breath. Let that calm linger as you settle down for the night.

Comforting Words
Everything you need is within you. Embrace your inner strength and know that you are enough.

Positive Affirmations
"I am calm. I trust my heart. I am at peace."

BEDTIME THOUGHTS

For Relaxation & Calm

My Prayers
Take a moment to connect with Grace and Love. Whether you believe in God, Angels, or a Divine power, know that you are lovingly watched over. Offer your prayers and feel the peace that comes from being heard and supported.

Simple Breathing Exercise
Breathe in slowly for four seconds, hold the breath, then exhale for four seconds. Feel your body relax with each breath.

A Short Visualisation
Imagine yourself in a lovely reading nook, surrounded by soft pillows and warm blankets. Enveloped in comfort, you feel secure and ready for sleep.

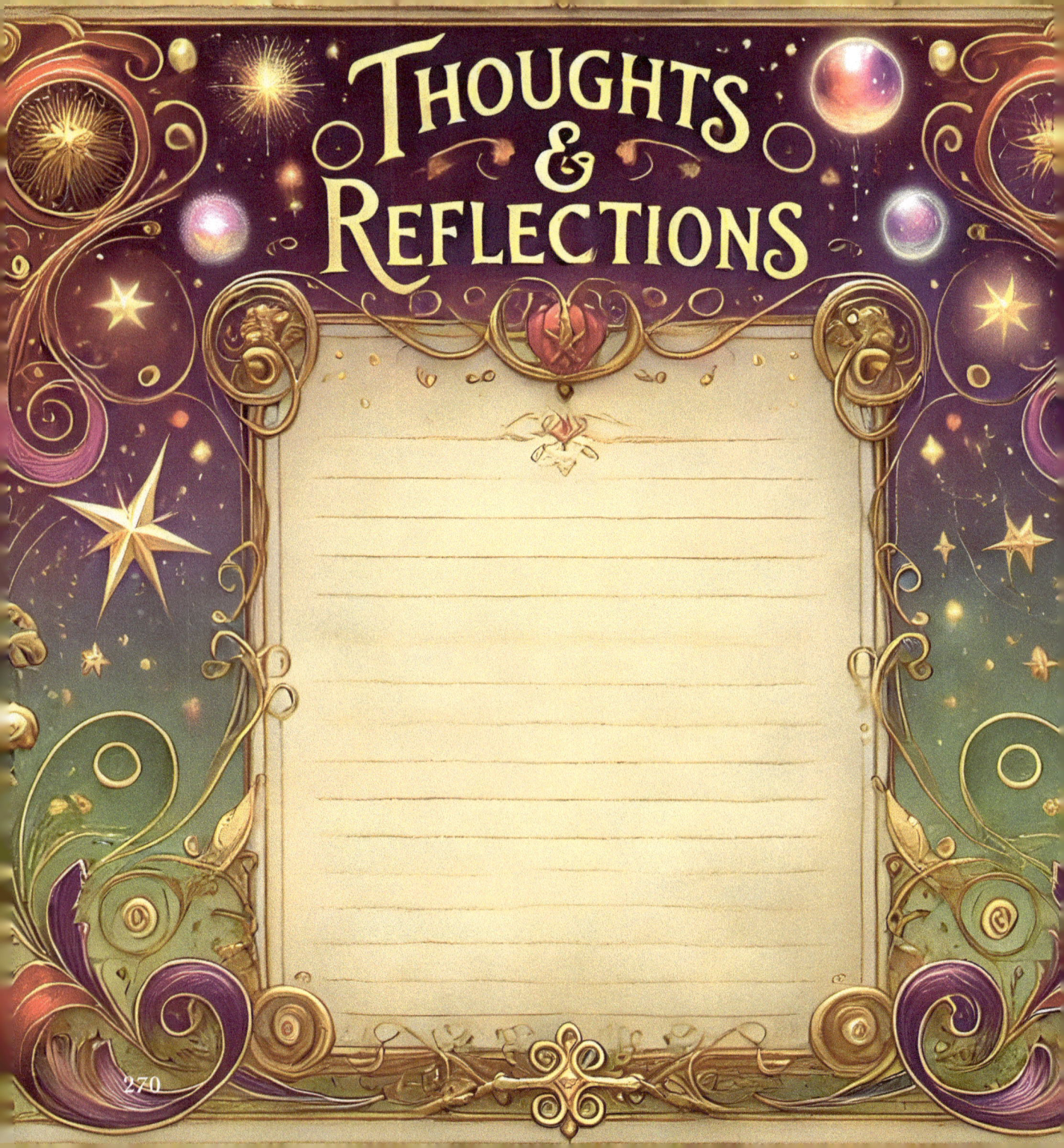

Thoughts & Reflections

My Dear Heart

You are always with me, always listening, always knowing what I need. You hold my dreams, my worries, my joys, and my questions. When I feel lost, you help me find my way. When I am unsure, you remind me of what truly matters.

I will learn to listen to you, to trust you, and to ask for your guidance. You are my friend, my safe place, my quiet strength.

Now, I will take a deep breath, put my hand on my heart, and ask, what do you want to tell me today?

Write your thoughts here or on a piece of paper.

CHAPTER 11
MINDFULNESS
RELAXATION &
MEDITATION

(For When You Need To Calm Down)

Opening Reflection

Sometimes, life can feel a little too busy or noisy, and you might feel overwhelmed or anxious. This chapter will introduce you to simple mindfulness practices, relaxation techniques, and meditation exercises that can help you feel calm and centred.

Emotion Wheel Activity

Now, take a moment to look at the section of the Emotion Wheel that represents how you feel right now. This can help you connect with your emotions and express them.

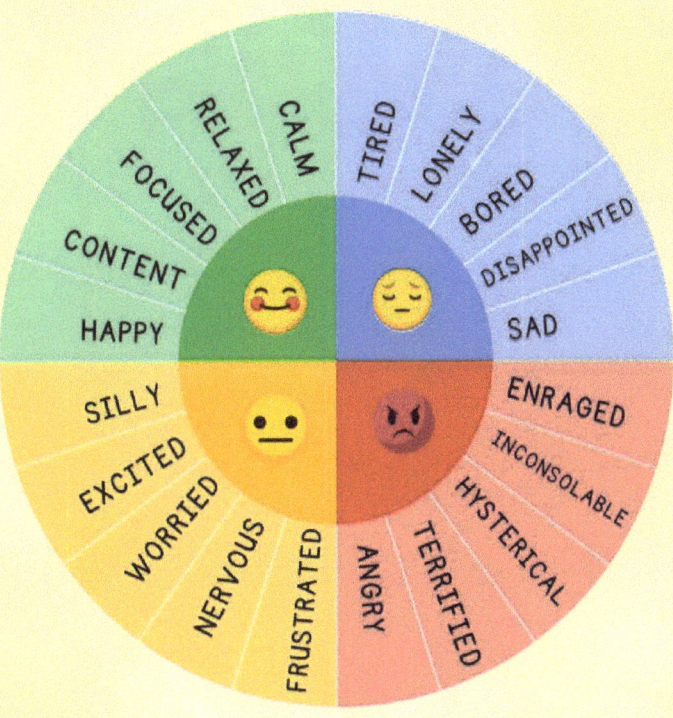

Positive Reminder:

Remember, Practising mindfulness, relaxation, and meditation can help you find calm in the chaos. You have the power to create peace within yourself.

How Do I Feel Today?

Take a moment to check in with yourself and write down how you are feeling right now? It is okay to feel a mix of emotions; whatever you're feeling is valid.

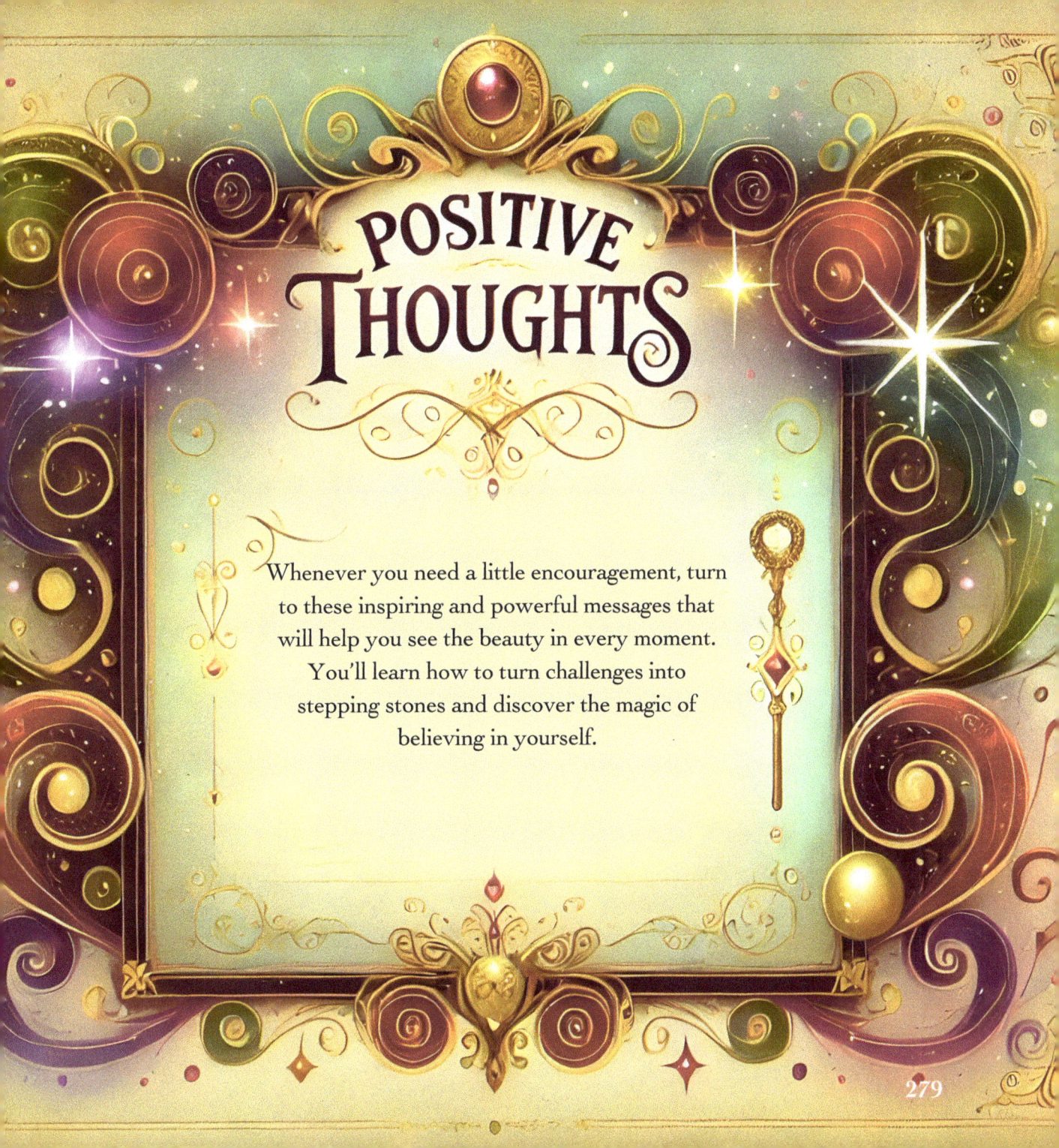

POSITIVE THOUGHTS

Whenever you need a little encouragement, turn to these inspiring and powerful messages that will help you see the beauty in every moment. You'll learn how to turn challenges into stepping stones and discover the magic of believing in yourself.

Positive Thoughts

1. Breathe In Peace, Breathe Out Stress
With each breath, imagine filling your body with calmness and releasing any tension. You can find peace within yourself.

2. Being Present Is A Gift
Focusing on the present moment allows you to fully experience life. Embrace the here and now and let go of distractions.

3. Your Mind Can Be A Calm Place
Just like a still lake, your mind can find tranquility. Take a moment to imagine a calm space where you feel safe and relaxed.

4. Feelings Are Like Waves
Emotions come and go like waves in the ocean. Recognise them, ride them, and know that they will eventually pass.

5. Nature Is A Soothing Companion
Spending time outdoors can help you relax and recharge. Notice the beauty around you and let it bring you joy and calm.

Positive Thoughts

6. You Can Create Your Happy Space
Imagine a place that makes you feel happy and safe. Whenever you need to relax, picture yourself in this special space.

7. Gratitude Brings Calm
Take a moment to think about three things you are grateful for today. This practice can help you feel more centred and at peace.

8. Your Breath Is Your Anchor
Whenever you feel overwhelmed, focus on your breath. It can ground you and bring you back to a state of calm.

9. Let Go Of What You Cannot Control
Sometimes, it is okay to let things go that are beyond your control. Trust that everything will work out in its own time.

10. You Are In Charge Of Your Peace
Remember that you have the power to create a sense of calm within yourself. Practice mindfulness and relaxation whenever you need it.

Affirmations

1. I breathe in calm and exhale stress.
2. I am present in this moment.
3. My mind can be a peaceful place.
4. I embrace my feelings as they come and go.
5. Nature helps me find tranquility.
6. I create my happy space wherever I am.
7. Gratitude brings me inner peace.
8. My breath anchors me to the present.
9. I let go of what I cannot control.
10. I am in charge of my peace.

Interactive Reflections

Relaxing Exercises:

1. **Five Senses Check-In (For Feeling Overwhelmed):**
   - 5 things you can see
   - 4 things you can touch
   - 3 things you can hear
   - 2 things you can smell
   - 1 thing you love about yourself

2. **Hand On Heart (For Comfort and Self-Love):**
   - Place a hand over your heart and close your eyes.
   - Take a deep breath in, then exhale gently.
   - Whisper something kind to yourself:
   - I am safe.
   - I am loved.
   - I am doing my best.

3. **The Worry Jar (For Letting Go of Worries):**
   - Find a jar, box, or envelope.
   - Write any worries on small slips of paper and place them inside.
   - Tell yourself, "I am putting my worries away for now."

Interactive Reflections

Journaling Prompt:
What is one thing you noticed today that made you pleased with yourself?

Friend Connection:
Invite a friend to join you for a mindfulness, meditation, and relaxation moment and share your best ways to relax.

Reflection Questions:
How do you feel after using mindfulness and relaxation techniques?

What is one new thing you learned about yourself through these practices?

Weekly Challenge:
This week, dedicate a few minutes each day to try mindfulness. Try different techniques and see which ones help you feel the most calm and centred.

Activity Page

Flutter & Float:

Get comfy and take a big breath in through your nose, imagining your tummy as a colourful butterfly spreading its wings wide. Hold that breath for a moment, then gently breathe out through your mouth, picturing the butterfly fluttering away. Repeat this a few times.

YOUR OWN AFFIRMATION

Write Your Own Affirmations

Ask My Heart

Your Heart Knows The Way

Deep inside you, there is a place where all the answers live, a place of kindness, and truth. That place is your heart.
It understands your worries, your dreams, and your deepest feelings.
When you're unsure, overwhelmed, or just need a friend, your heart is always there to listen.
Put your hand on your heart and take a deep breath. Your heart is always listening, always here for you. Whenever you need help, guidance, or just a moment of comfort, ask your heart.
Become friends with your heart, trust it, and share your thoughts and feelings.
Write down your questions, tell your heart about your day, and listen for what it has to say.
Your heart is your guide, always ready to help you find your way.

BEDTIME THOUGHTS

For Relaxation & Calm

Gentle Reflection & Gratitude
Think of a time today when you laughed wholeheartedly or smiled so deeply that your heart overflowed with warmth. Let that joyful memory fill every corner of your heart as you drift into a peaceful sleep.

Comforting Words
You are a cherished soul, uniquely beautiful and loved beyond measure. Embrace the gentle warmth of your heart, knowing that you are exactly where you need to be, surrounded by care and deep affection.

Positive Affirmations
"I believe in myself. I am following my dreams. I am happy with who I am."

BEDTIME THOUGHTS

For Relaxation & Calm

My Prayers
Take a quiet moment to connect with Grace and Love. Whether you believe in God, Angels, or a Divine power, feel the loving embrace that surrounds you. Offer your heartfelt prayers and let that sacred connection fill you with peace and comfort.

Simple Breathing Exercise
Take a deep breath in, hold it close to your heart for a moment, then exhale slowly like a tender sigh, releasing every worry and inviting serenity into your being.

A Short Visualisation
Imagine your heart bathed in a warm, glowing light, a gentle radiance that makes you feel loved and cared for.

My Dear Heart

You are always with me, always listening, always knowing what I need. You hold my dreams, my worries, my joys, and my questions. When I feel lost, you help me find my way. When I am unsure, you remind me of what truly matters.

I will learn to listen to you, to trust you, and to ask for your guidance. You are my friend, my safe place, my quiet strength.

Now, I will take a deep breath, put my hand on my heart, and ask, what do you want to tell me today?

Write your thoughts here or on a piece of paper.

My Dear Heart

My Notes

WELLBEING TIPS

Taking care of yourself is all about balance. Eating healthy foods gives your body energy, simple exercises help you feel strong and relaxed, and the power of your breath can kerp you happy and calm.

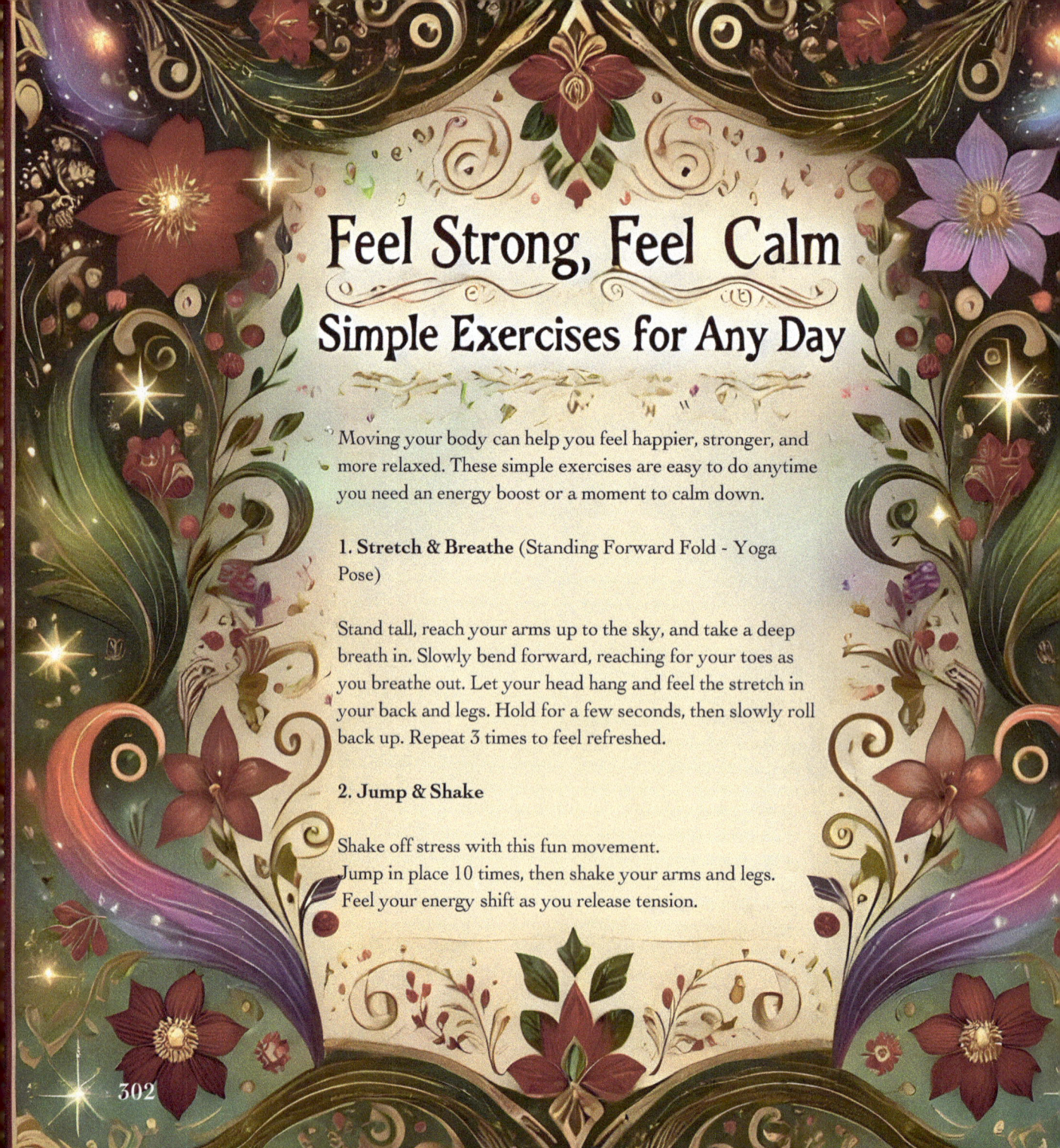

Feel Strong, Feel Calm
Simple Exercises for Any Day

Moving your body can help you feel happier, stronger, and more relaxed. These simple exercises are easy to do anytime you need an energy boost or a moment to calm down.

1. Stretch & Breathe (Standing Forward Fold - Yoga Pose)

Stand tall, reach your arms up to the sky, and take a deep breath in. Slowly bend forward, reaching for your toes as you breathe out. Let your head hang and feel the stretch in your back and legs. Hold for a few seconds, then slowly roll back up. Repeat 3 times to feel refreshed.

2. Jump & Shake

Shake off stress with this fun movement.
Jump in place 10 times, then shake your arms and legs.
Feel your energy shift as you release tension.

Feel Strong, Feel Calm

Simple Exercises for Any Day

3. Balance & Focus (Tree Pose - Yoga Pose)

Stand on one foot and place the bottom of your other foot on your ankle, shin, or thigh. Bring your hands together at your heart or stretch them up like tree branches. Hold for 10 seconds, then switch sides. This helps with balance, focus, and mindfulness.

4. Mindful Walking

Take slow, mindful steps, paying attention to how your feet touch the ground. Breathe deeply and notice what's around you, the colours, sounds, and smells. This helps clear your mind and relax your body.

Try these whenever you need to wake up your body, shake off stress, or just have fun!

THE POWER OF YOUR BREATH

Sometimes, a simple breath can help you feel calmer, more peaceful, and safe. These special breathing exercises use soft, gentle sounds, "Hu,' 'Hak,' and 'Hi" to help you let go of worries, relax, and feel good again. Whether you're feeling overwhelmed, need comfort, or just want a moment of peace, try one of these calming breaths. Take your time, listen to the sound of your breath, and notice how it makes you feel.

Did you know that your breath is like a secret superpower? It can help you feel calm, safe, and strong, anytime, anywhere. When you feel overwhelmed, nervous, or just need a moment to relax, try this method"

Whenever you need a moment of calm, try the **Hu-Hak-Hi Method** and feel the difference in your body and mind.

The Hu-Hak-Hi Method

Your breath has the power to calm your mind, ease your body, and bring you back to a place of peace. The **Hu-Hak-Hi Method** is a simple way to let go of unhappy thoughts, relax, and feel safe. Each breath has its own soothing sound:

Hu Breathing Exercise

Hu – A soft, flowing breath to clear your mind and to feel lovely.

Close your eyes and take a deep breath in. now, as you breathe out, softly say 'Huuuuu' (like the word who but stretched out). Feel the gentle vibration in your chest as you let go of any worries.
Breathe in calm... Huuuuu... breathe out sad thoughts and unhappy thoughts.
Try this a few more times, letting each 'Huuuuu' help you feel more peaceful and relaxed. Imagine your breath carrying away any upset and tension, leaving you feeling light and at ease.

Hak Breathing Exercise

Hak - A deep, releasing breath to let go of anxious and heavy feelings.

"Close your eyes and take a deep breath in as you breathe out, gently whisper or softly say 'Haaaak.' Feel the warmth of your breath as you release any stress or heavy feelings.
Breathe in peace... Haaaak... breathe out anything you don't need.
With each breath, imagine a soft breeze clearing your mind, leaving you feeling light, free, and ready for rest. Try this a few times, letting the 'Hak' sound help you feel safe and relaxed."

Hi Breathing Exercise

Hi – A light, gentle breath to bring comfort and ease.

Take a deep breath in, as you breathe out, gently say 'Hiiii' like a soft whisper. Feel the air flow out smoothly, carrying away any worries or tension.
Breathe in calm... Hiiii... breathe out stress.
With each breath, imagine a warm, golden light filling your heart, bringing comfort and peace. Let the gentle 'Hiiii' sound help you feel safe, relaxed, and ready for a restful sleep.

These simple breathing sounds: **Hu, Hak,** and **Hi**. Each one has a gentle rhythm that helps your mind slow down and your body feel at ease. Breathe in deeply, breathe out with a soft sound and let yourself feel lighter, more peaceful, and completely okay.

Healthy Eating: Fuel Your Mood & Body

What we eat affects how we feel, both physically and emotionally. Just like a plant needs sunlight and water to grow strong and healthy, our bodies need the right foods to stay energised, happy, and ready to take on the day. Eating healthy foods can help you feel better, both inside and out.

Here are some tips for eating healthy:

1. Eat A Rainbow

Fill your plate with colourful fruits and vegetables. Red apples, orange carrots, green spinach, blue blueberries, each colour helps your body in different ways. The more colours, the better. These foods are full of vitamins and minerals that help you stay healthy and feel good. Eating a variety of colours gives you more energy, helps you think clearly, and keeps your skin glowing.

2. Whole Grains Are Superstars

Choose whole grains like brown rice, whole wheat bread, and oats. They help keep you feeling full and give you steady energy all day. Unlike foods made with white flour, whole grains have fibre, which is great for digestion and keeping your energy levels balanced. Whole grains also help keep your mood steady, so you don't feel moody or tired after meals.

3. Protein Power

Protein is important for keeping your muscles strong and your body healthy. It also helps your body recover after exercise.

Foods like chicken, fish, beans, nuts, and tofu are great sources of protein. Eating protein helps your body grow and gives you energy to keep going strong all day. When you get enough protein, you can feel more focused and ready for everything, whether it's school, sports, or hanging out with friends.

4. Drink Water, Not Sugar

Water is super important to help your body stay energised and hydrated. Drinking enough water helps you focus, stay active, and even feel happier. When you don't drink enough water, you might feel tired or grumpy. Try to drink lots of water and cut back on sugary drinks like soda and juice.

Too much sugar can make your energy spike and then drop quickly, leaving you feeling tired or moody. Water helps keep your energy steady, so you can stay at your best.

5. Avoid Too Much Sugar
Eating too much sugar can affect how you feel. Sugar can give you a quick burst of energy, but it doesn't last long and can leave you feeling sluggish or irritable. Eating too many sugary foods can also cause problems like headaches or difficulty concentrating. Instead of sugary snacks, try healthy treats like fruit or yoghurt, which give your body natural energy that lasts longer and helps you feel good.

6. Healthy Foods Help Your Mood

What you eat can also change how you feel emotionally. If you eat too much junk food, you might feel sluggish, upset, or find it hard to concentrate. But when you choose healthy foods, your body can handle stress better, and you're more likely to feel happy, confident, and calm. Foods like fruits, vegetables, nuts, and whole grains can boost your mood and help you feel positive and ready for anything.

7. Listen To Your Body

It's important to eat when you're hungry and stop when you're full. Pay attention to how food makes you feel.

If you eat something sugary, do you feel good at first but tired later? Or does eating vegetables and fruit make you feel strong and focused? Your body knows what it needs, so try to pay attention to how you feel after different foods.

Take a moment to think about the foods that make you feel your best. What can you eat today that will keep you feeling energised and in a good mood?

Mindfulness is about noticing what is happening around you and inside you, like your thoughts and feelings, without judging them. Relaxation helps you unwind and let go of stress, while meditation allows you to focus your mind and deepen your sense of peace. Together, these practices can help you feel more balanced and happier.

Mindfulness Exercises

Mindful Stretching
Stretch your body gently. Reach your arms overhead, stretch side to side, and feel your body wake up. This helps release tension and brings awareness to how you feel.

Listen A Your Senses
Take a moment to focus on your senses. What do you see, hear, smell, and feel right now? Engaging your senses helps you stay present and enjoy the moment.

Imagine A Happy Place
Close your eyes and picture a place where you feel super happy, maybe a beach, a park, or your room. Your imagination can help you feel more relaxed.

Relaxation Techniques

Breathe In Calm
Sit comfortably and take a deep breath in through your nose, imagining calmness filling your body. Exhale slowly through your mouth, letting go of any stress. Repeat this a few times.

Nature Walk
If you can, go outside for a short walk in nature. Pay attention to how the ground feels beneath your feet and the sounds around you. This helps you connect with the world and feel calm.

Mindfulness Exercises

Find Your Special Spot
Create a quiet, comfortable space to relax. This can be a special spot for practising mindfulness and relaxation whenever you need it.

Meditation Practices

Guided Visualisation
Close your eyes and picture a peaceful scene, like a serene beach or a meadow. Imagine the sights, sounds, and smells. This practice helps clear your mind and fill you with calm.

Let Your Thoughts Drift
Imagine your thoughts are like clouds in the sky. Acknowledge them and let them float away. This helps you understand that thoughts come and go, allowing you to find peace.

Gratitude Reflection
Take a moment to think of three things you are thankful for today, like a friend or a special item.. This helps shift your focus to positive feelings.

Weekly Challenge
Try a new mindfulness, relaxation, or meditation exercise every day this week. Journal about how each one makes you feel. This challenge can help you discover which practices work best for you.

You Can Always Come Back To This Moment
Whenever you feel overwhelmed, remember that you can practice mindfulness, relaxation, and meditation anytime. It's like having a superpower that helps you feel better.

Your Special Message: A Reminder Of Your Power & Strength

Hi Amazing You!

Congratulations on finishing this book! You have embarked on an important journey of self-discovery and growth, and that is no small feat. By taking the time to explore your feelings and learn about your inner strength, you've already proven that you have what it takes to navigate life's challenges. This is just the beginning of a beautiful adventure, and your commitment to understanding yourself is something truly remarkable.

As you reflect on the emotions and experiences we've shared, remember that it's perfectly okay to feel a wide range of feelings: joy, sadness, fear, and excitement. Each emotion is a vital part of your unique story, like colours on a canvas, blending to create the masterpiece that is you. Embrace each feeling as a powerful teacher, guiding you through the twists and turns of life. You have the courage to face whatever comes your way, and every step you take is a testament to your strength and resilience.

Hold on to the belief that you possess incredible power within you. Just as a tiny seed can grow into a towering tree, you have the ability to overcome obstacles and reach for the stars. When faced with challenges, remember the strategies you have learned in this book: the magic of kindness, the importance of connection, and the beauty of self-acceptance. You have everything you need to rise above any storm and shine even brighter than before. As you step forward, know that you are worthy of love, happiness, and the dreams you dare to chase. Embrace each new day as a chance to discover your potential, share your light with the world, and inspire others along the way. Your journey is just beginning, and the best is yet to come.

My Notes

My Notes

www.ingramcontent.com/pod-product-compliance
Lightning Source LLC
Chambersburg PA
CBHW061157010526
44119CB00059B/846